TELLING MY STORY

THE HEALING JOURNEY - MEN'S STORIES OF RECOVERY FROM CHILDHOOD SEXUAL ABUSE

First published in Australia in 2022

Shooting Star Press

PO Box 6813, Charnwood ACT 2615

info@shootingstar.pub

www.shootingstar.pub

ABN 63 158 506 524

This collection copyright © GCASA

The right of the men to be identified as the authors of this work has been asserted by them in accordance with the *Copyright Amendment (Moral Rights) Act 2000*.

All rights reserved. Other than brief extracts, no part of this publication may be produced in any form without the written consent of the Publisher. The Publisher makes no representation or warranty regarding the accuracy, timeliness, suitability or any other aspect of the information contained in this book and cannot accept any legal responsibility or liability for any errors or omissions that may be made.

A catalogue record for this book is available from the National Library of Australia.

Telling My Story

ISBN: 978-1-925821-43-7 print

ISBN: 978-1-925821-76-5 ebook

Cover Art by Fred Thompson

Drawings by Fred Thompson and Jacob Tuton

Image by Elias from Pixabay

Design & Typesetting by Cath Brinkley

CONTENTS

Introduction ... x

1. A BOY FROM KALANGADOO ... 1
   Jim McNichol

2. TEARS OF A CLOWN ... 11
   Francisco Pangorva

3. ALWAYS BELIEVE THE CHILD ... 19
   Lance McKellar

4. THE PATH TO FORGIVENESS ... 27
   Joseph

5. FINDING FREEDOM ... 37
   Dustin

6. BREAK THE CYCLE ... 45
   Brian

7. THE COMET ... 53
   Peter

8. EVEN THE LONGEST JOURNEY STARTS WITH A SINGLE STEP ... 63
   Garion Potter

9. HEALING THROUGH SHARING ... 71
   Ross

10. BREAKING THE TABOO ... 81
    Stephen

11. BREAKING THE STIGMA ... 93
    Rex

12. RUNNING FREE ... 101
    David Nguyen

13. HOW DARKNESS BECAME MY BRIGHT LIGHT ... 111
    Mark Cooper

14. KEEPING GOING ... 121
    Tim Rose

15. THE RIPPLE EFFECT Kevin Whitley		131
16. FOLLOW THE YELLOW BRICK ROAD Brayden Crane (he/him)		143
17. LINE IN THE SAND Mal		155
18. WALKING WITH YOU Clinton Allman		161
19. THE DANCER Andrew Mournehis		173
20. INSIGHTS John Spender		179
Notes		187
Acknowledgments		189

"Once you choose hope, everything's possible."
Christopher Reeve

Some information, stories and experiences in this book may be distressing to readers. Please take good care of yourself as you read this book and if you require help or someone close to you is at risk of harm, please contact any of the following for support:

Respect: 1800 737 732

Lifeline Australia: 13 11 14

Sexual Assault Crisis Line 24-hour free call for crisis support line: 1800 806 292

Kids Helpline: 1800 551 800

Survivors and Mates Network (SAMSN): (02) 8355 3711

DEDICATION

To other survivors, everywhere and in all walks of life, of all ages,
Know that you are not alone.
Whatever happened is not your fault.
It is always possible to move forward in your journey.
Shift your perception, you deserve acknowledgement, the most important thing is you.
It's okay to lose yourself before you find yourself.
We stand with you and honour you.
If you stay silent, the darkness won't get any brighter.
We encourage you out of the shadows, help is easier to access than it was.
Reaching out started the process of healing for me.
Anything is possible.
It's your journey and it's personal, move forward with hope and vision.

INTRODUCTION

The stories within this book are a gift given to us by these men. They share their stories with purpose. Their words reach out to other male survivors to bring an understanding only they can give; to tell these men they are not alone and tell the boy inside he is not to blame. They share the power of telling their story, the positive impacts of having support and how this enabled them to move forward in their journeys.

Their stories speak to the challenges, stigma, and struggles of survivors, but also to the hope, freedom and healing. They acknowledge the personal and professional supporters, articulating the difference these people have made, and the valued support they continue to provide, to these healing journeys.

It is their hope that they can make a difference as they share with the community the reality for many men and the trauma that continues to be inflicted on young boys. It is through the sharing of these stories that society can better understand the impact of sexual harm, break the taboo and open up such truths about our community. These men, through their stories, challenge us all to question the ways society operates at all levels and create a better-informed and safe community to raise a child.

These authors are known to us all, they are sons and fathers, husbands and partners, friends and workmates and stand next to you and me. It is reported that 1 in 9 men (11%) were physically or sexually harmed before the age of 15 and many more go unreported. The true figure may never be known.

Recovery is a lifelong journey and is different for every individual, but there are many commonalities, many things they all share. The men in this book share candidly the impact on their wellbeing, emotional stability, and family relationships – and the isolation, shame, guilt and resentment that can ensue throughout these experiences. We are grateful that these men have trusted us to publish some of their most vulnerable insights. Moreover, the stories bring hope for all men touched by sexual harm that recovery is possible.

The strength and determination of the authors cannot be undermined, their stories are often traumatic, but they are also powerful. Hope and resilience shines through them all.

A BOY FROM KALANGADOO

JIM MCNICHOL

My life that surrounds me today started in 2012. I was fifty-eight years old; I am now sixty-five years old. There is a distinct difference between life pre- and post-2012. I have always been a loner; I would typically be the last one at a party to leave, provided there was something to drink. I was the one falling into a stupor drinking too much. I tried different drugs, but luckily, I never liked anything enough to continue. I have my good health, my marriage, my partner, my children, my grandchildren and my career. These are important to me.

Prior to my marriage I did not keep relationships for any length of time. I kept moving on. People ask me why I spent a long time, often in excess of ten years, in one job. I always felt safe in these jobs. When I felt this way, I stayed. When I did not feel safe, I moved on, whether from a relationship, a job, friends or acquaintances.

I am successful. I attained a Bachelors Degree of Commerce, am a Fellow of Certified Practising Accountants (CPA) and completed an Accounting Certificate (TAFE) with Honours. I worked up the ladder from storeman to chief financial officer (CFO). I have a beautiful family with a daughter and two sons, one from a prior marriage, and three grandchildren with a fourth on the way. I have been married for forty years. I value my children and my partner, and while I sometimes don't show it, the love I have for them is there. I am proud of what I have in life. However, I am not proud of the past, where I have been distant and not a part of the joy that my family have experienced. I cannot change that.

I began by saying my life as I know it now started in 2012. One night I awoke around midnight, I stood up from the bed, and thought, "Oh hell," remembering a particular time at school when I was told by my form master that they knew about "the abuse" and the abuser, he was going to be sent away. I did not know what to do with this memory of an event that I had not remembered before this night. I couldn't remember any details about the event or the abuse itself, only that I was told I had been abused.

Over time, memories came back. I remembered being in the school on a long weekend, alone. I was not able to go home to my family as other boys had. I presume it was because my parents were separating around then. I found myself intensely trying to work out what happened, the event's timeline, and determine who abused me. The abuser was always a shape in the shadows.

In April 2012 there was the Victorian Parliamentary Inquiry into the Handling of Child Abuse by Religious and Other Organisations. When I looked for the start date of this inquiry for the purposes of including it in this written account of my story, I started shaking and I felt tense and uneasy. I realised that my memories surfaced at the time of this inquiry. It was also the time of my fortieth high school graduation anniversary. I did not graduate at Year 12 as I was expelled partway through Year 11. At the time, my subconscious mind was relieved that I was getting out of the school, out of the fire and somewhere safer.

Initially, when I recalled my experience it felt like I was outside my body, looking down on this child being sexually abused. Later, I experienced memories of laying down, being abused. I came to know when and where the abuse occurred, the memory of going through the doors into the laundry and into that small dark room with high windows. I recognised the mattress on the floor and the bookshelf. I still do not remember who abused me, despite seeing the outline of the person nearly every day. I remember the smell of the laundry. The rough unshaven face touching me, his hands pulling me to him, the memory of what he made me do and what he did. My mind is still keeping me safe from going further.

I question whether I need to know what actually happened. My inquisitive mind says "I do" but my adult self says, "So what? I don't have to know. It was bad and that's enough. I am safe now." I know I tried to fight back and I froze. I tell myself it was not my fault. It was his fault – and the institution's for removing the problem by expelling the troubled teenager who could not be controlled, rather than dealing with the actual situation.

I learned about and rang Victoria Police's SANO Task Force but I hung up. I did not have the courage to speak up and I had not told anyone about my memories. I was dealing with it on my own.

In 2013, the Royal Commission into Institutional Responses to Child Sexual Abuse began. I made a promise to myself. I was standing in a car park, ready to go into the gym. The Royal Commission announced that registrations for private sessions closed at 5pm that day. It was 3pm on the 30th of September, 2016. I told myself if I do not register for a private session in that very moment, then I would be forever silent and not tell anybody. I know that phone call saved my life.

I was nervous, sweating, and my heart was running at a million miles an hour. A woman answered the phone. I answered the questions. Was I sexually abused? Was it within an institution? What was the institution? When did it happen? Do you know who abused you? I felt relief that I did not have to say what exactly happened. There was no denial about the abuse from the woman on the call. She believed me. She said I was brave. I said that I did not feel brave. I felt scared. I told her rather than the word brave, I thought the word that she mentioned – "resilient" – best suited me. I had survived and I had a future. I now had a plan to progress.

I was advised of the process in telling my story to the Royal Commission. There would be redress. An apology from the institution. I would have contact with the police. The woman asked me if I wanted to be provided counselling. I said, "No, I'll be okay, no worries."

I told the woman she was the first person I had spoken to about my experience. She was not surprised and said many others had also not told anybody before. I had waited fifty years. Many others had waited much longer to tell their story. I now know why counsellors ask, "What are you going to do now?" and, "What is coming up in the next few days, weeks?" They want to know that you are safe. The woman asked me these questions once she decided that I fitted into the box of experiencing institutional child sexual abuse.

I continued to go on as I had. I tried to deal with the issues I was having by myself. I received emails from the Royal Commission, advising counselling was available should I want it. I was still working out exactly what had happened to me. I could work this out on my own. I felt that I could not talk to my family about my experience. I felt that since I was a man, these things don't happen to men, or if they do, we take them on board and tell no one. I questioned how I would let someone do this to me and how I wouldn't fight back enough to stop it. I blamed myself without knowing it.

In December 2016, I decided to tell my family, because I

could not hide the fact I would be involved with the Royal Commission. While walking through a shopping mall just before Christmas with my wife and daughter, I felt safe that I could share my experience without feeling trapped. I told them I had been sexually abused as a child at boarding school and I wanted to be involved with the Royal Commission. My wife and daughter responded supportively. I then called my son, who, while shocked, was very supportive. While I felt huge relief, my family did not know how to console me. I still felt embarrassed for my experience and for not standing up to my perpetrator.

I downplayed the seriousness of the abuse with my family and there was silence about it, as nobody seemed to know how to talk about it. I could still deal with my experience myself. I was strong. I just had to wait; I could tell my story and then get it out of my mind. I just had to go through the steps of the Royal Commission and get it over and done with.

The black dog came. The doubts. The anger. The thoughts of not having to deal with life. The ideas about being in a peaceful place. To commit suicide. I had my steps in attaining redress and an apology all planned out, and then the thoughts would come on like a freight train running through my mind. I thought that I was strong enough and resilient enough to deal with this. I was so, so wrong. In early 2017, after spending Christmas with my family, I realised I was not strong enough. I was resilient but I also needed help to survive. I would not be able to tell my story unless I called for help. The devils in my mind were procrastination and pride. I just needed to make that call.

I made a decision which saved my life. When I rang, I was told somebody would contact me. I thought they would realise I was in trouble and needed help, and I would get a call quickly. Three weeks later I rang again. They responded with, "Sorry, we were going to give you a call when we had an appropriate counsellor to contact you, and they only just started in their job this week." It was a close call. I was about to give up.

I came to realise through counselling how much the enormous emotional swings I experienced were connected to my abuse, and I learned that no child should experience abuse, nor are they responsible for it.

In sharing my story, almost all, either have presented as consoling towards me, or have shared their own experiences with me. I gauge other people's reactions closely before sharing my story to see how they will cope with what I am going to share. My siblings, nephews and nieces, work acquaintances, counsellors, psychologists, psychiatrists and doctors all know my story and I have become aware of others' experiences of abuse as well. In 2017 I told my doctor about the abuse and he gave me a referral to see a psychiatrist. The wording on the referral said "Victim of Historical Sexual Child Abuse". It really hit me then I had to get more help so that I could continue to be a survivor, not a victim.

I wanted to find out where I fitted in and if other people were on a similar journey to me. I found a men's survivors group and got the courage to attend their programs. I enjoyed being part of a group that consisted of all male survivors of different ages and backgrounds. I learned to talk to others, rather than keeping things to myself where it can take over my life and reinstate the perpetrators' message about "tell no one" or "don't tell". Find someone to speak to whom you have faith in and trust. If the first time you tell someone, it doesn't work out well, don't despair – try again. You will succeed in finding the person who believes you and can help.

Know that not all people are bad. There are people out there who will want to help us. We are not alone. It may be a long journey, but you will survive. When the wave of helplessness overcomes you, understand why it happens, get out from under it and rise above it. We cannot take back what has happened, and it is in the past. Everything that you do to move forward takes the power away from your perpetrator and brings it back to you.

Being believed has been a huge part of my journey to recovery, and I have always been believed. Being brave and speaking out has been the hardest part for me. I now share my story so that people can recognise when things are not alright – and they too can speak up and protect both themselves and children.

Every story we tell spreads out like nutrients that are absorbed into the roots of a tree. This is the tree of knowledge that absorbs the information so that more and more people are aware. This awareness grows in momentum, so that we as a society can create change. We must help those in recovery to move forward. I am proud being one of nearly 10,000 people who told their story to the Royal Commission. That afternoon in the car park, I hoped that there would be change and it has been greater than I could have imagined. It began with telling my story.

I am still understanding why and how this happened to me. I don't think the healing process will ever end, as I still deal with the thoughts coming up. My life is now one of not letting these thoughts control me in the present. I have learned the past can haunt you, but cannot hurt you.

I want children to know they have power, and to understand they can speak up and tell someone about what is happening rather than letting it lie as long as I did. Even though I'm an adult who can access help, my inner child sometimes comes back as a frightened little boy. These days we have great support networks ready for us. Sometimes it may feel like being at peace is a better option, but this would then transfer the despair on to those who love and respect us. My family and mental health are now the most important things to me. Even still, there are times where it is still very hard and I fall into a hole.

I was handed a poem by Portia Nelson with a line: "I walk down another street".[1] The author speaks about walking down a path and falling into many holes along the way, and having the option to choose another street. I have fallen down the holes that Nelson talks about, and still chose to walk down the same street. This has been my insight: to notice what doesn't work and to remember we have the choice of where we walk. There may be other options available to you if you put in the work to find them. The most important thing on the street is you, remember that. It is you.

NOW

Love came. I still have my bad days
I can choose to no longer allow my trauma experiences to define me
I'm in control of how I react and respond
I am able to remind myself to think of the bigger picture
You can overcome the experience and live a worthwhile life
I enjoy giving support, to help other survivors in any way possible
The impact that I am making through helping other men is no longer small
My brain wiring has changed in a healing way, maintaining my sense of being
I have arrived at where I wanted to be, I am and can more fully be a loving father, a husband, a son, a brother, an uncle....
I hope I get to meet you on your journey

TEARS OF A CLOWN

FRANCISCO PANGORVA

Leaving the bathroom, battered and bruised, four women stared at me with a glaring look of cold disapproval and obvious judgement. "They must know," I said to myself, as they gave me the same disapproving look after he quietly "led" me into this strange bathroom. "They must be disgusted with me." The shame. I've not only let myself down, but yet again, I've obviously let my family down and clearly deserved what happened to me.

Walking home was slow-paced, but I wouldn't have known; my head was assessing what just happened, as I played all of the roles of judge, jury and jailer. Instead of fighting or running, I complied like a lamb being led into a slaughterhouse. I clearly deserved what happened to me.

As the youngest of seven children to a mother with only six teats, as a child I had never felt "seen" by those who mattered most to me. So I became the stereotypical "problem child", craving attention. Adding to this, I had been diagnosed with ADHD and dyslexia; I was labelled by my teachers as both "dumb" and as a "bad egg". One Year 5 teacher even suggested that I be sent to a special needs school.

Living up to this unenviable label was always difficult for me, as I never felt like a "bad egg". But my parents were of a generation that "one doesn't question authority" and I know it bothered my academically minded father thinking his youngest was "thick". Uncertain as what to do, my father decided to send me to live with my maternal grandmother. As the matriarch of my large Latino family, and as a headstrong woman herself, if anyone could "straighten me out", it was her. So while walking home in this haze of shame, I replayed all of the times that I caused angst with my parents, teachers, and older siblings. This was why this evil happened to me, because shit like this doesn't happen to "good eggs".

Opening the door to my grandmother's home, I was late for dinner, she approached the front door and looked at me. I sheepishly looked to the floor so that she couldn't look into my eyes. And yet, part of me was relieved as she'd surely hold me lovingly, telling me how things would be okay. Instead, however, she gave me her usual stern stare and said, "You got into another fist fight? When will you STOP being such a disappointment to the family?" I can't recollect what else she said after this as I yet again fell into a state of disassociation, as if I was floating like an astronaut within the darkness of Alice's rabbit hole.

She sent me upstairs to shower without dinner. As I showered, with the hot water stinging my sores and raw anus, I turned this physical and emotional pain into a moment of personal reflection. If indeed I deserved what happened to me, then it was up to me to change. Instead of seeking attention by being the bad egg, I would focus on being a better student, son, and person. I would overcome my ADHD and dyslexia, and hopefully capture favourable attention by being the "good egg".

As the years passed, with my improving grades and sportsmanship I pushed on towards university, post-graduate studies, and a white collared career path. My focus was to "succeed", albeit by a definition given by society, rather than my family (let alone myself). My focus on growing into a "man" was orchestrated from a textbook – I worked long hours, putting any spare energy into learning and even more work. I was gaining my family's attention, but the one I sought it most from, my father, was mired with the onset of his dementia. The more that I climbed, the more his dementia and old age made it difficult for him to recognise my achievements. It was like scoring a goal to a fan base clapping with only one hand.

By the time I was in my thirties, if you'd given me a lie detector test while questioning me about my childhood trauma, I would have passed when I said that it was nothing more than someone trying to seduce me as a boy. This lapse in my traumatic memory did, however, ultimately serve a purpose: it allowed me to keep myself focused on my career and being a more deserving person. But my challenge, however, was that the higher I climbed, the emptier I felt. Not only was my father unable to see me with praise following his onset of dementia, but I felt no fulfilment from climbing this corporate ladder.

I had a life that many would envy: a good home with a wife and children. I was a devoted father. Like all fathers, I was protective. But this protection took another level, inasmuch that I was a guard dog who was being walked by the two children. Rather than looking after my own kids, I was looking out to those coming towards my kids. I no doubt annoyed my family as I presented as overbearing and controlling. I wanted to let go and let them live, but this was as foreign to me as learning an unknown language.

Control to me meant safety. I later learned that this control wasn't me controlling what they did, but placing limits on what exposure my family had. Yes, I know, it's still controlling. My concern was looking outwards rather than looking towards them. Not that this mattered, as all "control" is still suffocating nonetheless. I read books and took classes on "active listening" and better parenting. The more I tried to learn to let go, the more frustrated I got due to my inability to do so. I didn't appreciate this at the time, but this was reminiscent to my own sense of failure as a son, only now it was presenting in my role as a parent.

While I was meant to be in the position to be very pleased with my professional progress, this meant little to me I was not experiencing growth as a person outside my professional role. Could it be that I was wrong? Could it be that my focus in being "better" was misdirected? Eventually, it was this unfulfilled and empty feeling which became my downfall. Like a stellar black hole consuming a universe, this feeling began to eat away at the emotional armour that I used to deflect the pain from my childhood trauma.

As a child, I felt unseen by my parents, and as a parent, I felt unseen as a father. In both cases it wasn't the fault of my parents nor my own family; however, it was on me as to how I manoeuvred my own growth on my terms. Cliché as this may sound, it does take personal strength and self-belief to have others believe in you. Only in my case, I had no self-belief, and therefore I felt unseen. It was no fault of anyone else, but my trauma slowly started to chip away at my armour until eventually it crumbled. Like white ants eating timber, eventually the emotional timber cracked and broke. And when it did, a flood of emotions that I had not felt since I was a boy engulfed and consumed me.

Taking a train to the city, and for the first time since I was a traumatised boy, I heard the same negative voices inside my head. Like nails to a chalkboard, these voices were piercing and mind-numbing. I fell into a dissociative mental state. Getting off at my station, I found myself standing still on the platform. I wasn't moving towards the stairs, nor was I looking to board another train.

Somewhere between getting off the train and walking on

the platform, the voices had convinced me that my family would be better off without me, that my failures would eventually cause them harm and pain. I emptily walked towards the end of the platform, where the northbound train enters at full speed. I stood on the side waiting for the next train to throw myself in front of. I was calm, albeit lifeless. The voices had won.

I could hear a train approaching. Walking towards the edge, I could hear a faint voice which had put the dark voices on mute. "You're better than this. You are not the failure that you think you are. All that you'd achieve is relieving your grief by passing this same grief on to your family." As a father who'd swallow broken glass for his children, hearing this was enough to pull me back off the edge of the platform. Seconds later, the train swished by with a gust of air that felt like waking up from a bucket of cold water.

I went outside the train station, sat at a coffee shop for what seemed like thirty minutes, and then I was asked by the barista if I wanted something for lunch. I was ill. I didn't have the courage to tell my family, but I knew I needed help. I turned to a friend whom I knew had strong empathetic traits. She listened, held my hand, and reassuringly told me that I would be fine. She said that she'd help me to find a therapist, and off I went, reassured that I wouldn't do this again and that I would seek help.

Like looking for new shoes, it takes several attempts to find the right fit. I found a wonderful medical psychologist, who after my third visit suggested that I see an eye movement desensitisation and reprogramming (EMDR) therapist. She felt that my subconscious was hiding something; the same subconscious which gave me the strength to be a "better son". She explained how EMDR is used to uncover traumatic events, whether they are car accidents or, in my case, child rape. After my second EMDR session, the floodgates were opened. Like pressing the play button on a recorder, I relived my trauma, only this time through the eyes of an adult with their feet in the present.

Wish I could say it was easy, but it took six or so months for the full story to come out; from how I was lured and "groomed" into walking with him into the bathroom, to the faces of these five women, to my grandmother, to my sleeping with the butcher's knife under my pillow from fear of the child rapist finding me again. And while I wasn't quite "cured" from my depression and post-traumatic stress disorder (PTSD), I was able to label my emotions when times became difficult. Even during my bad dreams, I could feel that part of myself psychoanalysing what the dreams meant, even while I was asleep.

My EMDR therapist and I discussed my joining a support group for men who had been sexually assaulted as boys. I joined a therapy support group with six to eight other male sexual assault survivors. I remember my first session; we all looked at one another as though our own story was unique. After a few sessions, where we slowly peeled back our armour, we could recognise the wounds we each held. While our stories were different, our wounds were near identical. A camaraderie was formed, like former prisoners of war (POWs); we each understood one another's story. We could all relate.

Feeling stronger, and able to understand both my trauma and my desire to be "seen" and appreciated, I knew that I had to do something for myself. With my wife and children all busy with their own academic studies, if there was ever a time for me to branch out and find myself, this was it.

The corporate ladder no longer meant anything to me. I no longer equated being "seen" with achieving professional success. I had no idea what this meant, other than knowing that staying on this professional ladder was no longer an option for me. Given that I had others reporting to me, I equally didn't want to let them down. So I went to my boss, sat down with him in his office, spilled my soul, and told him that I needed to resign. As scary and foreign as this was to me, at no point was I feeling that I was making a mistake. And given my boss was himself a thoughtful and empathetic soul, he understood and was equally supportive.

I freely admit that my hard work and professional focus allowed me the luxury to go on my "spiritual gap year": hiking in South America, walking the 800km of the Camino de Santiago (Spain), camping in Israel, volunteering at an elephant sanctuary in Thailand, and circumventing Tibet on a motorcycle. I found myself in dangerous situations, where my only thought was surviving. While I'm still working on my self-esteem and worth, I know that it is improving. While I still find myself regressing every now and then, I am able to look through the dark moments, and approach loved ones for help. I am stronger now than I've ever been. But equally, I know that I have a need to be even stronger and more self-aware. This path of mine still has far to go, but looking back, I see just how far I've marched.

In short, I've come to learn that the trauma does not define who I am. I define who I am. I define my own ambitions and myself. I move forward with hope and vision. But if and when I do regress, I am confident to know that I will hit many hands when I extend mine for help.

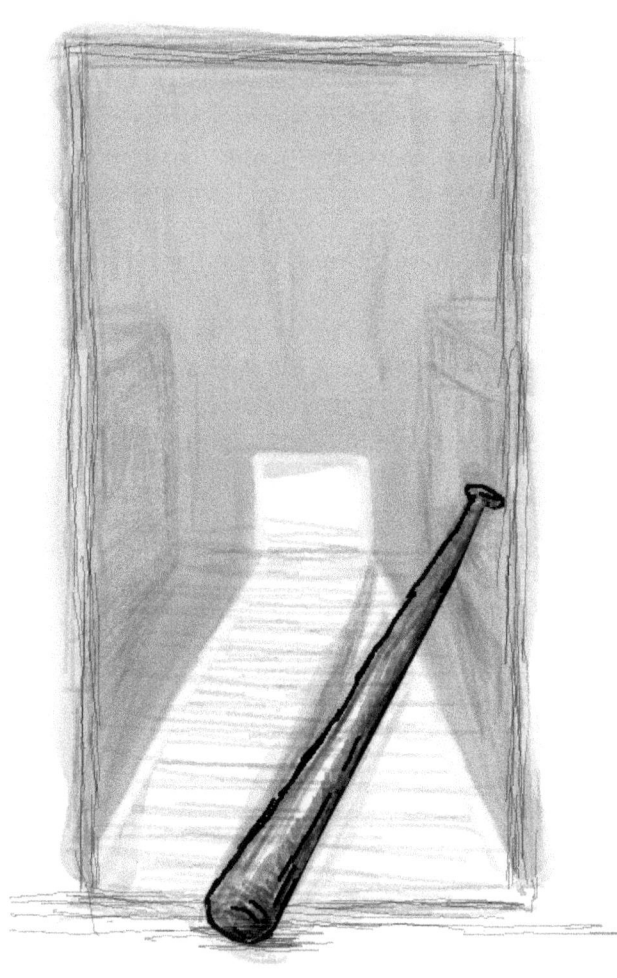

ALWAYS BELIEVE THE CHILD

LANCE MCKELLAR

I wrote my experience using a pseudonym and in the third party.

Lance was born in the metropolitan area of Victoria. He is the son of teachers and he has an older brother. His first experience of sexual abuse involved an encounter with a young man in a park. Lance was looking for cicadas when he was approached by a stranger. While Lance told nobody about the incident for a number of years, it continued to affect him. Beginning with self-harm and banging his head; later in life, he would experience sexual confusion.

Soon after this initial incident, Lance witnessed two teachers having sex and he confronted the male teacher about what he had witnessed. Lance was sexually abused while the female teacher banged his head against a wall, telling him that he was "just a girl". This caused self-harm issues and this incident would not be reported to police for many years, even then no further action would be taken.

In his family life, Lance grew up feeling like he was never good enough. Around a similar time of the abuse incidents, Lance had a judo instructor who placed him up against older and more able-bodied students, the instructor wanting to attract the best students for his new martial arts school. Later in the year, the death of the family cat, who had been placed inside a polystyrene box with holes punched in it during a family road trip, further impacted Lance's resilience.

Each of these events took place over one year in Lance's life and greatly impacted his emotional and psychological wellbeing.

Lance was educated at a private school with his brother, where they both experienced teasing by the other children. As a child Lance's brother had fallen from a tree house, which resulted in him experiencing brain damage. One particular experience of teasing which greatly affected both Lance and his brother was when a child spread a rumour that Lance had pushed his brother from the treehouse.

For fourteen years Lance was part of a church-run organisation for boys which, for the most part, was a highly positive experience for him. There was, however, one dark experience on a camp in 1983 where Lance was molested by two camp leaders and a third person, who knew Lance's father through their shared profession. Lance had witnessed a boy being molested by one of the leaders and after confronting the leader about this, he was fed a mouthful of flour and punched in the guts by a number of other boys on the camp, at the behest of the leader. The sexual assault occurred that night. At this point, Lance silenced himself on his experiences of sexual assault.

Some years later, Lance became a camp leader himself, although he struggled with church politics and was kicked out of the organisation. One night in 1989, a leader who had a prominent position in the organisation came to the church for a visit; he and another male taunted Lance about molesting boys. Lance became concerned about the safety of the boys on the camp and he stayed up overnight so that he could oversee their safety. Lance held a baseball bat up to the leader and suggested that he leave. The leader was soon exposed for his behaviour. In adult life several of the boys thanked Lance for protecting them.

ON LANCE'S return to the private school, he was again sexually assaulted by another student on four occasions, and physically assaulted over the course of his nine-year education at the school. Following the sexual assaults and emotional taunting by both adults and other children, Lance experienced poor self-esteem; he believed that being raped was his punishment for being weak. Lance believed that speaking out was a sign of being even weaker.

After sexual assault allegations against several teachers at the private school were aired in 2015, Lance contacted the school. Subsequently, he went to the police and a former student was charged. Following a review of Lance's case, all four charges of indecent assault were dropped in 2018. The former student had been jailed twenty years earlier as a convicted paedophile and two of the perpetrators from camp convicted and jailed of other offences.

After finishing university and experiencing unemployment during a recession, Lance returned to cleaning which he was involved in as a student. For years, Lance was in and out of work, where he suffered from workplace bullying. Lance experienced the failure of several business ventures and a property investment go wrong, which resulted in him losing his house. Lance lost further tens of thousands of dollars through a conman and blackmailer and found himself working many unsatisfactory jobs in order to earn back money. The police eventually caught up with the blackmailer, who managed to beat the charges against him. (This person died in 2016) In 2009, Lance found that he was burnt out.

Lance was referred to a men's support group for male survivors of childhood sexual abuse by his social worker, and things improved somewhat. Within weeks, Lance felt that the blackmailer was out of his life and his recovery began. In 2009, Lance appeared in a documentary for male survivors of sexual abuse and he became involved in several avenues of support for other survivors.

Alongside this, Lance, now married with a daughter, experienced bankruptcy and had to move house, but found he was not eligible for rentals given his financial status. After relocating, his family then had to move three times in three years. The family's housing instability created friction with Lance's in-laws. Lance took on work cleaning and again tried his hand at setting up a business. At one stage the business was going well; however, Lance was also ripped off by a subcontractor. Changes in the marketplace, problems with staff and a bout of hepatitis in 2017 took their toll and later, as the result of Lance losing his driver's licence, he was forced to sell his business (cleaning shop fronts). Lance was now in his early 50s and somehow seemed to end up at 'the bottom of the heap' in life, time after time.

After becoming involved in failed attempts to join volunteer organisations and a Meetup (mental health) support group, Lance worked as a courier for a while. Dismissed from his job things quickly went downhill. Several interdependent relationships turned sour. Covid struck and made things worse!

At the time of writing Lance is working part time as a cleaner in addition to receiving a Disability Support pension. Lance has been diagnosed with mental health and complex cognitive disabilities. He hopes to return to study in the field of community service. Joining a Men's Shed, NDIS therapy and a walking group has been beneficial. Lance has taken up art again. A number of classmates from school were supportive once the abuse was disclosed and the boys who Lance protected at the sleepover expressed their thanks to him. One response was so moving it had Lance reduced to

ALWAYS BELIEVE THE CHILD

tears! Lance has had the chance to share his experiences at two Royal Commissions.

Lance wants other survivors and those supporting them to take on the following messages:

1. Don't blame yourself
2. Always believe the child
3. Just because someone else has a similar experience, this does not mean that your journey will be similar to theirs
4. Learn what your boundaries are and stick with them
5. Be brave in telling the opposite sex about your experience
6. Never tell someone with lived experience to "snap out of it" or "get over it" – they've got to move through it, which includes finding acceptance in their journey
7. No matter what happened, always report it to the police
8. Perpetrators are both male and female – there is no stereotype.
9. I have found out who my real friends are, and I was always believed when I shared about my experience.

AUTHOR'S NOTE: the above experiences are mine and are written in the third person, to help me cope. I will conclude with one story. At a forum for survivors, the question was asked, "Should you believe a child who says they are being abused?"

I rose to my feet and said one short answer. "Always believe the child!" You could not hear a pin drop in the room.

Thank you for reading my story.

CONTEXT OF ABUSE

Every child assumes their family is normal
The family unit had been broken for a long time
Everyone in our family was certainly damaged in some way
And all types of abuse existed in our family
There was an unspoken rule of silence around strongly held emotional subjects
Domestic violence....broke my childhood. This was when the abuse started
I was painfully shy and I did not make friends easily
Lonely, self-conscious, introverted, I strove to fit in
I was a submissive child, who bowed to authority
I felt unseen by my parents
I grew up feeling like he was never good enough
I became the perfect subject for opportunistic paedophiles.
Was I sending them signals
I was always very caring and thoughtful
And I never told a living soul what'd happened to me
My childhood innocence was violently taken away from me
I felt dirty and violated
I was just an innocent child
It affected me more than I could possibly imagine

I had been self-medicating on drugs and alcohol in different forms since I was 12
I had my suspicions that I'd been abused
I feared no-one would believe me
Victims are groomed to remain silent
....I wish my parents told us about saying "No".
As far as I'm aware, it was never reported
It finally struck me that I had in fact been abused for all those years.
There was a part of me that knew what was occurring was clearly wrong
As victims, our voices are taken away
We suffer shame, humiliation, embarrassment, anxiety and feelings of inadequacy
We often lock away those dreadful memories of the past into the deep, dark oceans of our mind
It's so important to allow yourself to grieve the loss of your innocence and allow a healing relationship to occur with your body

THE PATH TO FORGIVENESS

JOSEPH

The two little girls smile and laugh as my wife and I enter the home. They are my granddaughters by marriage and it is not an every-week visit, but when it does happen it is very special! Where we live, around 6am, it is an early start for us with a morning walk. Thirty minutes of exercise to feel ready to get into the day and to help our blood pressure levels! For me, it's a little easier in the warmer seasons, whereas when you know the air will be cool it's hard just to put the gear on. I am able to convince myself that the invigorating start to the day is good for me. We are in our sixties now and still both work part time, and while we are keeping ourselves comfortable, it is a struggle, just like it is dealing with the past.

We live quite frugally, which is a necessity for us and it makes me feel that I am a responsible person. There are times when I am tempted to break out of this routine, but I am able to remind myself to think of the bigger picture. We socialise quite regularly with our friends, who are Filipinos like my wife, and they are such happy, positive people it is always an enjoyable experience.

JOSEPH

My experience of sexual abuse was a one-off event. Just a couple of years ago I was a part of a men's group and I found it to be extremely shocking to hear the other stories of repeated abuse. Despite this, the one attack on me by a close family member was followed by psychological abuse which continued for a period of time I am unable to specify, as my defence was to block it out of my mind. What I can do, though, is link it with the downward spiral in my school learning. I was about twelve years old and I had been near the top of my class in terms of academic achievement each year. In fact, probably about a year before it happened I was the dux of my class at my new school. We had moved house that year, to a new suburb very close to the beach. Once the abuse started and even when it stopped, I withdrew and I had no interest in learning. This continued for the rest of my schooling years and into my adulthood.

When the incident of sexual abuse occurred, I froze and I did not make a sound. With the psychological abuse that followed on for some time, I did oppose it. I took solace in listening to music, playing football, and going to the beach; they were the three things that consumed me! Once I finished high school, I was offered to take a scholarship and study at a teachers college. Without giving it much thought, I accepted the opportunity to live three hours from home. This, of course, meant that I would spend a lot less time with my perpetrator.

Being separated from my perpetrator wasn't really in my thoughts at all; I was focused on going off to work with a great group of people! In reality, I became a social alcoholic, drinking myself into blackouts on many, many nights. When I was back in my home I didn't drink; it was only when I went out with friends. Being with a group of friendly, wonderful people at college was a saving grace for me.

When I finished college and I returned back home, I was

lost! I avoided forming any long-term relationships with women because I was scared. I didn't marry until my early thirties, which was to a strong, but dominating and controlling woman. Eventually I felt so trapped, like I had been almost thirty years beforehand as a child, and I did nothing to stop our marriage from failing.

When my abuse had occurred many years earlier, I really did not know what to think as my perpetrator was a family member. I guess that I was in complete mental and physical shock.

I felt completely helpless when it happened because I was the much smaller person. I can't remember anything that happened before it which could point to such an attack occurring. I don't even remember if it was dark or light in the room. The abuse itself didn't seem to last very long, and when it reached the point of intense contact, I opened my eyes because before that I had pretended I was asleep.

I don't know if the psychological abuse started soon afterwards or if there was a big gap, but I believe that I felt trapped. We were in the same room; he could behave and act how he liked and I was at his mercy. I don't recall ever thinking that I should tell somebody about this; in fact, I didn't tell anyone what had happened until about twenty years later. Of course, in school back then we didn't have a counsellor. It's almost like I was ashamed of what happened; I guess I made an unconscious decision to keep it to myself. A few years later, my perpetrator told me that he would tell others what I had done!

As I got older, it all stopped. Maybe he was smart enough to realise that I might take him on physically. I know that in my late teens I definitely harboured resentment towards him, and I would try to make eye contact with him with hatred in my eyes, but he didn't notice.

I have had two people in my life who have helped to

restore my hope and I am so grateful for their support. I met the first person after the disintegration of my first marriage. My first wife never knew about my abuse because I never told her about it. We had difficulties in our relationship; when I look back, I now believe that if I had opened up to her, we would have had a better relationship. My wife brought safety, calm, kindness and, most importantly, unconditional love to our relationship, which was something that I had never experienced beforehand. I was a heavy drinker when we met, and this changed, partly because she drank very little, and also because I didn't feel the need to drink as much when we were together. My wife taught me to be happy, positive and sensible – which, when I look back, I had not really been before this time.

Tragically, our relationship was cut short when my wife contracted a terminal disease. I was devastated, and while I didn't turn to alcohol to help me resolve my emotions, I instead turned to other addictions. For the most part, these didn't make me happy at all – apart from my penchant for golf, which made me very happy!

The second person in my life who has restored my hope is my current wife. I opened up to her a lot further about my experiences when we first got together, after beginning a long-distance relationship. She is also a happy, positive person who lights up my life every day that we are together.

I feel that the response of people around me to the events that I have experienced was stymied because I have not divulged very much information to those closest to me. By accident only a few years ago, one of my siblings became aware of my past as I referenced it in a Facebook comment and they saw it. However, apart from an acknowledgement and an apology for this happening to me, they haven't raised it with me again.

My partners who knew of the sexual assault haven't offered to talk about it further either. I believe it is difficult for people who have not experienced sexual abuse to comprehend the magnitude of the devastating effect that it can have on a person. Ironically, while I said very little in general in my first relationship about anything, my current wife believes that I talk too much!

I have spoken to several counsellors over the last twenty years or so and they have all been very helpful to me in different ways. I believe that I could have achieved even more out of counselling if I had shared more with them, as no matter how much I would talk, I still felt like there was unfinished business. I guess that's partly because the journey of recovery is lifelong. My counsellors responded with outrage when I recalled the events of my assault and I found that this certainly helped me immensely, because it gave me recognition that this shouldn't happen!

If I could speak to someone else who had experienced something similar to me, I would tell them to make sure that they work with a counsellor to talk about their experience. Tell the counsellor everything, especially about your feelings. I didn't do this until many years later and it resulted in many difficulties for me as I became a teenager, and then an adult. It is much better to talk about your experience when it is clear in your mind. A counsellor will be able to give you strategies to employ in your life so that you can counteract the difficulties that may arise. This alone will give you a sense of hope.

The counsellor will be a support person for you; they will have experience working with others who have also been through abuse. You will feel positive and hopeful when engaged with them, knowing that you can overcome the experience and live a worthwhile life. You will be able to recognise and understand your own sense of hope, which will help to guide you throughout the years. I didn't have this guidance for so long, meaning that I had further trauma in my life which didn't need to occur if I had sought help when I was younger.

I would like to assure other survivors that it is always possible to move forward in your journey. What has happened is truly appalling and we cannot change this, but we must also accept that there is no blame at all attributed to us. It will take much effort, determination and persistence on our part, and the support of others; we cannot heal on our own. I am an example because I tried to do it on my own for a long time, but without addressing the situation my life never really got on track. The hope returned once I sought help.

We need to help make the community more aware of sexual abuse because many people may think it would not have happened to anyone they know. I am sure they would be surprised to learn how common it actually is and that there is a very good chance someone they know has been sexually abused. Many of my friends, family and countless others who I have come into contact with don't know my story because I have locked it away. If you are prepared to open up and find ways to do this that feel comfortable for you, sharing your story can be a constructive process.

My healing from my childhood abuse is not finished; the healing process is ongoing. I have moved from locking it away to having quite regular thoughts about it; I have been sad, lonely and depressed, but also circumspect and hopeful. Right now I am contemplating telling my family about the abuse that I have experienced, almost a half a century and most of my lifetime after it happened. While I have thought about sharing my story with my family for some time, I want to speak to a counsellor first.

From here on, I want to continue to find happiness in my life, which becomes easier when I make sure I take my depression medication, and when I focus on the good things in life. My hope for my family is that hearing about my experience will have a positive outcome and that we will all become better and more loving people as a result of it. However, I am also aware that they are each likely to have different reactions. I also hope in my heart that I can find forgiveness for my perpetrator, because I'm not there yet.

THE QUESTIONS….AND THE RE-LEARNING

I have always sought answers
I was looking myself in the eye and asking seriously difficult questions
How would I show my children what it is to be a man?
What did this mean for my sexuality? For my masculinity?
What would the other kids at school say?
What would my family say?
Was I sending them signals?
Why would my body respond like that?
And what about that dreaded idea about victims of abuse becoming abusers?
In time, you'll come to know that this is a process of unlearning
And sometimes, what we don't know is, our greatest strength will be found in our weakest moments
So give yourself the time you need to process what comes up
There is no blame at all attributed to us, so be gentle on yourself
Allow yourself to be supported by others
We've all had a lot of knockbacks in facing our inner demons,
We still do sometimes, but we kept going
Try not to bury yourself in guilt and anguish for the choices and manipulations of another human being

A new, reconstructed self who will never be as we were before can emerge.
We're much further from where we started
We can tell our self, that little boy inside, the man we are today, that we love him
We can tell him that it's always possible to move forward in our journey
To fight with all that you have, all the strength you've got
We didn't die, and we've been able to build a life
And we are, essentially, okay
We are still strong. We will never be broken
And we walk with you, we all walk together

FINDING FREEDOM

DUSTIN

*H*ello, my name is Dustin. I'm thirty-six years old and grew up around the treetops of rural Victoria as well as having a great upbringing on Victoria's coast.

I'm a qualified and seasoned chef in the hospitality industry and I have been fortunate enough to work my way up to the top tier of the industry. My career has taken me all over the world. I have trained in some incredible venues and under some amazing chefs, and I have developed some invaluable and priceless skills along the way. I love what I do!

I have a passion for Brazilian jujitsu, yoga, movement, meditation, personal development – and I fucking love food, and I'm going to swear a bit more throughout this story.

Twenty-five years on from where this story starts, I'm grateful for life, clean water, my family, my home and everything else that my life has provided for me. As my dad would say, "At least nobody's shootin' at ya."

You'd think that life's pretty good when you're working on a million-dollar boat on the French Caribbean, making heaps of cash with no budget. It would sound mind-blowing, right? Not so much.

Out of respect for the victims who have been so unfortunate to experience the vulgar and disgusting behaviour that is sexual abuse, I'm going to state first up that I was not sexually abused to the full extent of some unfortunate others who have been significantly abused, molested or even raped. I would call it being sexually mistreated or misconduct, and my experience was more around a combination of scenarios. While most kids should have been playing in the yard, building things and living the joys of a childhood upbringing, I was living in fear. The fear of getting in trouble and the fear of getting told off for something that was happening next door.

When I was a young lad I was keen and eager to jump into the world of work and making my own money. I found good cash work at the slaughter yard next door to our house when I was around ten years old.

I would generally spend my Saturdays hosing shit through the floors of the holding pens out the back – but every now and then, when there was a day off school, I would go down to the abattoir and work on the floor. I worked in all sections of the processing plant. It was somewhat like a normal job. There was a lot of foul language, sexualised verbal trash and plenty of insanely rude (and funny) jokes, but mostly filthy talk that you'd expect from a bunch of bogan slaughterers.

I felt like a cool kid. I was working, I could buy things; I had independence.

This was until my eleventh birthday, when the boys thought it would be funny to turn me upside down and hang my head over the bloody pit, joking that they were going to dip my head in because I was mouthing off. I ran out of the slaughter yard crying that day. I never told anyone about it. I also never told anyone about the daily visions of blood and guts spilling onto the yard floor, the sound of screaming, the helpless (and at times abused) animals, the smell of urine and the nature of the death zone. This was certainly enough to give a young boy nightmares.

There was a guy who lived on the property of the yard. We became friends. He used to watch snuff or rape films. I used to break into his caravan and watch them while he wasn't there. I thought I was pretty tough. There were a couple of incidents when he would ask to see my penis. I showed him once, and he touched it. He ended up trying it twice.

I didn't think much of all of this for a long time. I dealt with the nightmares of the slaughterhouse and we moved away, so I never had to see him again, and nobody would ever need to know. I told myself that I would be fine.

What had happened didn't really hit home too hard until I was about twenty-two years old. I was working as a young apprentice at the time, with many hours a week. While I watched my friends get messed up, go out, shag girls and cause trouble, I was working like a dog and becoming resentful, jealous and angry, feeling like I'd drawn the short straw on life.

Throughout my career, I continued to work as a chef, pushing my problems down, firing on all of the youthful resources that I could access. My mantra became "just keep pushing and eventually you'll turn the page and it'll all go away". I worked like fuck. Sixty, seventy, one hundred hour weeks, back to back for days on end. I worked 113 days straight once "piling cash", but still I was in stupid amounts of debt.

I stayed in this pattern for a good fifteen years until I popped. I was burnt out in a big way. I had exhausted every resource I had through smoking weed, drinking, trying to health-kick, late nights, parties, distractions. I was cooked. Physically, emotionally, spiritually – also known as completely fucked.

To top it off, I was also angry.

All of this generally ended in me screaming at a loved one randomly and screaming at myself in trauma. I pushed like an animal, a slave to my thoughts, hoping that it would all go away. I imploded. I was fucken over it. Life held no value to me. And I was supposed to be the one who did well.

Out of respect for those who chose to take their lives through suicide, I still wanted to be alive. Although at times the thought was hanging by a thread, I still saw light – I still felt loved.

It's no wonder that chefs hate their careers so much. What an intense whirlpool of processing emotions stuck inside a 50-degree stainless steel hotbox of chaos led by the sound of extraction fans.

And on this note, Anthony Bourdain[1], we honour you.

I remember one night after I felt "self-rejected" about a girl (who was in a relationship). I drove home blind drunk at 130km with no seatbelt on, not giving a fuck if I crashed or not. I woke up the next morning alive, unharmed but with a deep feeling of self-induced sadness.

"What the fuck am I doing with my life?"

I had to change. My family loved me unconditionally, I had friends, I was good at stuff and I must live. I knew of a couple of old hippy healers in the bush and this is where I went to begin my inner work.

In the last eight or so years I've turned my emotional mission control system inside out. I knew the path to happiness for me was in emotional healing. Not only did I have the prick who touched me charged, but I forgave him as well. I had started to peel back the layers of the onion. Now would also probably be a good time to tell you that it wasn't quite as easy as I thought it would be. It took longer, and I went deeper.

When I decided to start this journey of self-healing, I was leaving no stone unturned and I was going to face everything, even myself. I knew that it would be worth it, I didn't know why – but I knew I had to start. I knew that I could experience a life that I had seen for others and resented. I wanted this for myself, so that I could share it with others. That was my mission. I needed to learn emotional intelligence. I wanted to become an expert at it, and I wanted good health. I believed that this was how I would help myself and others, and I was gonna be a man about it! I am going to set myself free!

(Tip for the reader – "Understand not what happened, but what you made it mean.")

As mentioned, I had met a couple of hippies who helped me to start this journey of healing. This couple really stripped the heavy shell that I had on.

This was my introduction to emotional intelligence, and embodiment. I have been involved in a wide range of practices and techniques: Chinese medicine, yoga and Ayurvedic medicine, chakra work, singing bowls, reiki healing, neuro-linguistic programming, hypnosis, the landmark method, inner child work and sexuality workshops. They are all worth a go.

When I finally understood that I didn't need to go into the stuff so much when I concentrate, self-care and nourish my scared, sad and shameful feelings, everything started to integrate. Through my journey over the last few years I've met many amazing facilitators who do amazing work and many great participants who are willing to be coached. There are so many people out there now doing this work and options are fruitful. Just ensure you read the product descriptions carefully.

When you feel lost or get stuck, be grateful, ask for help, find love, and give it warmth.

Practice presence.

I could use another whole page explaining the amazing journey that I went on with different healers and facilitators, and inspiration that I discovered along the way, but I don't think that that is what is going to be most helpful. What will be helpful is some foundation work.

So, here are some key principles to think about:

- Find a good coach and healers. I have found about seven to ten who are qualified in their own field of expertise and I see them when I need them. They cover health, personal growth, Chinese medicine, body and muscle support, business mentoring...
- Find a movement practice that you've always wanted to do. Practice your new practice.
- Get as strong as fuck.
- Get grounded. Processing your emotions needs movement. Yoga, martial arts practice – exercise even in the smallest capacity or use meditation. Just do something.
- Eat like a champ. Having a good, healthy, nourishing diet will give you the fuel you need to get awesome.
- Show up for yourself.
- Cry your eyes out. Do it in love and in pain.
- Be grateful. Even in the hardest of times, it helps.
- Buy karma points. Become a volunteer doing something you enjoy.
- Come back to your practice. Falling off is not a worry. Gently remind yourself to get back on the bike. There is gold everywhere.
- Keep going!

I feel in a lot of ways that I have overcome the trauma of my experience now. I have taught myself some amazing self-help tools, I'm now a coach myself and I have a great foundation for self-sustenance and working ecologically. I'm an eager business owner and my goal is to continue to grow myself and my business to encourage growth in others.

My new mantra is "If you want something you've never had, you've got to be prepared to do something you've never done."

Thanks for reading.

Peace. Love. Light.

BREAK THE CYCLE

BRIAN

My name is Brian and I am sixty-one years of age. I am married with two boys who are aged eighteen and twenty-two. Family is important to me, and it always has been from when I was a very young boy. I have a small group of friends, several of whom are also survivors of sexual abuse. I am a more reserved type of personality, so I don't feel that I need to have a multitude of friends. However, I like company and having close friends is very important to me.

The sexual abuse started very early in my life. I would have been five years old at most. In fact, all types of abuse existed in our family from as early as I can remember, particularly psychological and emotional abuse. I know for certain that one of my sisters was sexually abused, and she was emotionally abused into adulthood. I suspect that my other sisters were also abused sexually. Everyone in our family was certainly damaged in some way.

My father was an alcoholic since as early as I can remember, and my mother had a multitude of problems, not the least of which was hating us with a passion.

BRIAN

I have always sought answers as to why circumstances were as they were, both from an external and an internal point of view. I guess I have always been in the right frame of mind to accept another person's guidance on how to "return things to how they were". Because of this, I sought psychological advice since I was a teenager. I would read psychology books to find an analysis of myself, and hence an answer to my current state of experience. As I became older, I sought professional help without knowing exactly what I was asking for. I at least felt that I was trying to change, and so I maintained some hope that there was the chance of recovery in the future.

My experiences of abuse left me with daily feelings of isolation, helplessness, shame, and a heavy depression. But as survivors would understand, I put on a mask and presented myself to the world every day. I got myself through secondary school in this manner, despite having a breakdown in Form 6. Essentially the family unit had been broken for a long time, and I never had anyone to confide in or talk to about my experiences.

I initially did not take ownership of these problems when I was young and it wasn't really possible for me to comprehend what was happening at that stage. I dissociated from an early age to cope and I also engaged in a pretty strong fantasy world. This does not lend itself to a foundation for recovery, so I began to pursue a lot of behavioural changes.

Throughout both primary and secondary school, I achieved well. Thankfully, I was blessed with a high level of intelligence, and I was always in the top few of my class each year. This was extremely important to my self-esteem and confidence, because without that I would have struggled with my level of worthiness. As I got older, sport was an emotional and physical refuge for me. Any awards gave me some energy to continue having hope and some belief in myself.

These abilities, while they gave me some pride, self-respect and kept me connected to the world, also masked the emotional void that I was experiencing.

While I was in Form 6 I had a breakdown that destroyed my chances of going to university, which was a passionate dream of mine. I was simply too ill to do anything at that stage. What this did leave me with was a burning determination to revisit this period of my life and "right the wrongs".

After the end of my schooling I eventually left home, which proved to be one of the most beneficial things that I did for myself at that point in time. I felt that I had a chance to breathe, since I wasn't experiencing abuse on a daily basis. I managed to get a job based on my Form 6 results, and I was grateful that I at least had a job. I still found life to be a massive struggle though.

I continually strove to fit in, in part because I placed a large emphasis on getting married. I eventually met someone and after a normal courtship, we married.

Soon, I began to think of the missed opportunity to go to university. It burned deeply. I knew that I couldn't become a doctor like I wanted to be in the first place, but I thought that I would at least create a career through accounting, and provide my family with some security. I entered university as a mature age student and I completed my part-time accounting course over six years. After that, I studied for another two years and I obtained my Certified Practising Accountant (CPA) qualifications. With great satisfaction, I at least felt that I could handle university and higher education, and it took away my feeling of failure after my earlier experiences.

I felt that marriage would also have some magical effect on my psyche, and that I would be able to leave my past behind. Unfortunately, I had seriously misjudged what recovery actually meant, because marriage certainly wasn't a panacea for personal ills. Hence, a time of self-reflection ensued for a period of my life. When I thought I was going backwards, I was really looking myself in the eye and asking myself seriously difficult questions. I can only say thank goodness that I did. This culminated in me one day looking up a number to call for support around sexual abuse. This was at the same time that I turned fifty years old.

Why this happened at fifty, I am not sure, but they do say that life changes when you are fifty. For me, I think that my life started again when I made that phone call. I have now been receiving sexual abuse recovery therapy for eleven years now. I think I can now say that every day is another day of recovery, with seemingly new experiences every week. I have changed from just talking about the abuse, to talking about what I need to do today and tomorrow in order to be a better person.

This has enabled me to be a better father and a better husband on a daily basis, which is extremely important to my sense of self and identity. Ironically, I thought from an early age that these values would be the foundation of my life, so here I am now finally living those values. I now have support from my fellow survivors, and I also enjoy giving support when this is needed. This is because there are still bad days and we are there for each other. Recovery is about being whole and recovering from the abuse that shatters our sense of self.

If a young person who had experienced something similar to me sought my advice, I would say several things. I would tell them that it's important to know that recovery has to be done at your own pace, and it is an individual process. It cannot be measured against any other person's recovery.

You will learn that the experience of abuse does not define you and you are not responsible for other people's actions. You have your whole life ahead of you; your circumstances will only improve with good help.

Importantly, trust your instincts and your gut feelings. These can disappear with the abuse, because you may lose all trust, including your trust in yourself. But when you do the work, life becomes an experience, not a daily struggle.

VALUES

Family is important to me, and it always has been, as are having close friends
Over this time I have found out who my real friends are,
And it was these real friends who always believed when I shared about my experience
I learned that not all people are bad
And together, we, as a society, can create change
We can all become better and more loving people
And create the kind of safe families and communities we needed
Helping is at the core of who I am
I practice life-long learning with regards to the impact of male child sexual abuse survival
My strength and my voice are lent to others that are yet to find theirs
I recognise I can't save everyone
But I want to do whatever I can to prevent abuse occurring to another child
This is my job now, this is my purpose
....to bring men of all ages out of the shadows and to break down the stigma surrounding male victims of sexual abuse
It's okay to fail at times, we all do. And never blame yourself

It's okay to stop or fall down sometimes. Keep going because you're worth it
I embrace all of myself, including the wounded and the "normal" parts
I lead by example, and I show my scars
I appreciate all that I am and all that I have
I'm grateful for life
I've come to understand that the most important thing is....you
I have found my purpose in life: to be here in this moment

THE COMET

PETER

I am a sixty-two year old male, married with two adult children who enjoys sport – particularly my Tigers (AFL) – music, and pretending to be a rock star. These passions, and the general hubbub of work and home life, have largely been my focus until late in 2017.

WHERE IT BEGAN

My father died in a pedestrian/motor vehicle accident when I was just four years old, and being the youngest child by over twelve years, it was just Mum and I in our housing commission flat from the time that I was eight or so. I was sexually abused around August or September of 1975, when I was fifteen or sixteen, by a teacher (a former clergy member) at the Catholic school that I attended. I idolised him as he was tall, athletic and it was rumoured that he played league football before coming to our school.

There were four instances of abuse. The first was in our school sick room, followed by two in the perpetrator's flat, and then finally in my home while my mother had gone out on a date on one particular evening. Prior to this evening, I had been severely concussed while playing cricket with friends a week or so earlier and had been absent from school since that time. After this incident, I "faked" having double vision so that I could avoid returning to school for the rest of that year. The perpetrator made one further visit to our home while my mother was present a week or so following the third incident, and my mother thought that this was wonderful of him to visit. For over twenty years, my feigning of the symptoms of double-vision was the dominant, if not sole memory, of that time.

As my school did not go past Form 4, my absence led to me missing the enrolment to continue at the senior campus and I relocated to a state high school in 1976. I was a truant for the first four weeks of the 1976 school year; eventually the school contacted my mother and I was brought into line. During my latter teenage years, I was painfully shy and I did not make friends easily. I still find this area of life challenging.

I was always a shy, submissive child, who bowed to authority. My mother was, I now believe, suffering from depression. Because of her fragility and my fear of (and submission to) authority, I told no-one and kept this secret until 2013, when I first told my wife.

I had no idea that others had also experienced abuse, as there was total silence and secrecy at the time of the incidents. I felt that I could not come forward, as I was shy, had a sense of shame, and feared that I would not be believed. I thought that it was partly my fault, and I also feared the effect this would have on my mother, who was quite religious and held the church in high regard.

I waited over thirty years to tell ANYONE. This is because I was fifteen years old at the time. Because he was my hero. Because he was my teacher. Because I thought I'd be expelled from school. Because I feared that no one would believe me. Because I thought that suicide was easier than telling even one person. I felt that being a man, I wasn't ever supposed to tell anyone about what happened. I felt that I would be viewed as weak if I spoke.

The Effects

I have hidden the abuse for my entire life and I have always had difficulty in dealing with conflict. My wife says that I become quiet, run away and hide rather than resolving confronting situations, which I have learned recently is my default unconscious reaction to feeling threatened. I wasn't even fully aware of the extent of child sexual abuse, thinking I was the only one, until my mid-thirties, by which time I had already been through my first episode of severe depression in 1980 at the age of twenty-one.

For a period in my late twenties and thirties, as I was having my own children, my own experiences were not at the forefront of my thoughts. I underwent a period of depression in late 1999, at the age of forty, which led me to have a short period off work and to change my job.

In 2001 my wife was diagnosed with breast cancer and the stress that the family underwent at that time brought on flashbacks of memories, which I was able to dismiss for a period of time.

In 2004, I again suffered severe depression, which lead to a six-month period off work while I underwent treatment and took medication. At this time, I had many thoughts of self-harm and worthlessness. I was able to resume work in March 2005; however, I remained on medication and under the care of a psychiatrist until 2008.

It was at this time that, as a part of my recovery, I again found my passion in music and I became a customer at a local music store. The owner of the store had attended the same Catholic school as me some years after I had. Upon learning that I had gone to the same school, they mentioned the name of my perpetrator, as he had become infamous. The mention of his name sent a chill through me, and this was truly the beginning of me piecing things together for myself.

In 2013, I again suffered an episode of severe depression. I was required to take medication under the care of my long time general practitioner (GP), but I was able to remain at work this time. I decided to tell my wife about the abuse and I sought psychological counselling in an attempt to deal with what was happening for me. At this time, I also learned that my perpetrator had abused other children and had, in fact, been moved to different schools TWICE before I encountered him. This discovery caused further pain and anger for me as a result of the callous actions of the Church and those in power.

In November 2014, I collapsed in tears at work and immediately went home. At this time, I again had suicidal thoughts and feelings of worthlessness. My GP immediately referred me to a psychiatrist and, through medication changes, I was able to return to work in late February 2015. I remain under psychiatric care to this day. I am on medication and I am relatively stable.

The episodes of news regarding the Royal Commission into Institutional Responses to Child Sexual Abuse over the past few years, and the seemingly regular revelations worldwide since, have always brought me to a place of deep sadness and anger on each occasion. Sadness for the lives affected, many far more seriously than mine. Anger at the lack of justice for all survivors and the ongoing disdain shown to them by the institutions that clearly, through their actions, value their wealth far more highly.

In 2016, I seriously considered speaking to the Royal Commission and, around this time I came across a prominent church leader in the street outside my work. This leader within the Catholic Church, right in front of me, out of the blue, was a triggering symbol of that institution and their behaviour. It literally stopped me in my tracks, anger welling up, until he left by car. To this day, I still have a picture of an advertisement inviting submissions on my phone. At the time, however, the hospital that I worked at was relocating to a new facility and I was exceptionally busy. Unfortunately, I did not revisit the advertisement until submissions had closed. This is a regret that I still hold.

The release of the report of the Royal Commission in December 2017 became the catalyst for my latest period of depression. In particular, the public response of archbishops in Melbourne and Sydney to the recommendations heaped further abuse on survivors, leading to more hurt and anger for me. I decided, in conjunction with my psychiatrist, that I was finally ready to fully confront the abuse.

I was referred to a specialised sexual assault service and, through them, I saw a psychologist with extensive experience in dealing with victims of sexual assault.

The Restoration of Hope

Over the years as I coped with my bouts of depression, and learned of the sorry history of abuse in the Catholic Church and other institutions, a great anger grew in me. Despite this, I did not act to confront the abuse and simply dealt with each set of symptoms as they arose, in the hope of maintaining a sense of normality. I see now that this was counter-productive for me, as it did not truly deal with the underlying cause. I was not able to build resilience and mechanisms to deal with issues as they arose, which could possibly prevent each mental health event from becoming serious.

I had always doubted myself because I could not remember specific details. It was only through my specialist sexual abuse counselling that I learned how the brain and memory works in a traumatic event. I now understand why I don't remember things like addresses, exact dates, and the full details of the abuse. While my memory of parts of the attack itself are vivid and detailed, there are still gaps, sort of like a film reel with only every thirtieth frame visible. I see his hand where it should not have been, my fear that I would be hurt, the feeling of anxiety and being unable to breathe.

This is a feeling that returns when my mental health begins to deteriorate. I have learned that apparently this is what happens: Your memory snaps photos of details. Details that will haunt you forever, changing your life and living under your skin. It doesn't record other parts of the story that really don't seem to matter much, or you cannot process due to the continuing trauma.

In the months immediately prior to my specialised counselling, I began to see that my anger on its own was destructive. It could dominate my thoughts and paralyse me, leaving only bitterness and sadness. During my first few counselling sessions, we developed a goal to move me from feeling like a victim to a survivor, one where the abuse and its effects do not dominate my life for large periods of time anymore. The key, for me, was to turn my anger into what I now call good, useful anger that can be used productively.

While I can never undo what has occurred, I can turn my anger into action to fight injustice.

I remain unconvinced of the sincerity of the Church, and indeed ALL churches and institutions, in dealing with these issues. This continues to inflict pain and engender anger for me. Instead of letting this anger well up and consume me, I now act and write to politicians, sign petitions and donate both money and my time to causes which seek to redress injustice in all of its forms.

Appalled at the way politicians were portraying them for political purposes, I have made the effort to meet, and now call friends, a number of African refugees. I can now speak in support of them with personal knowledge and will always stand with them as they suffer racism and vilification. I have volunteered as a mentor for refugees seeking work in Australia and this has been exceptionally rewarding. When I see a shy immigrant's joy at reaching their goals that they thought were impossible, and they can see that there are many Australians who welcome them to our country, I know that I am contributing in my small personal way to making this world a better place.

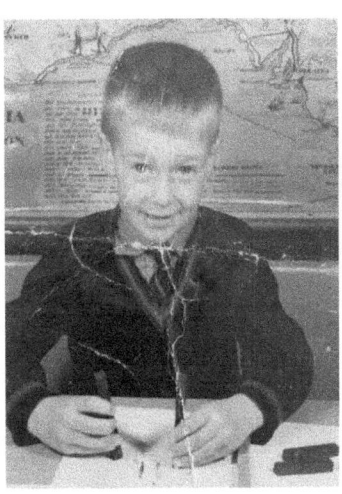

I ENGAGE with international survivor groups through social media because I want to do whatever I can to prevent abuse occurring to another child – or to ensure that, if it does, they know how to speak up and that they will be believed. I also extend this to female survivors of sexual abuse in its many forms. Women must also be believed and supported; as men, we are best placed to address the attitudes which lead to violence against women by calling it out whenever it appears.

. . .

Final Thoughts

For anyone who has experienced abuse, know this.

It was not your fault.

You did not deserve it.

You will be believed.

You deserve acknowledgement, contrition and justice.

While the effects of the abuse will always be with you, it can grow to be like a comet, only appearing briefly with long periods out in the cosmos where it is not affecting you.

> *After the violence came the shame*
> *With the shame came the silence*
> *With the silence came the pain*
> *With the pain came the anger*
> *But with the anger, I found my voice again!*
> Anonymous – Twitter, circa 2017

IN THAT MOMENT

I felt completely helpless when it happened
The abuse itself didn't seem to last very long....I had pretended I was asleep
I was in complete mental and physical shock
I don't even remember if it was light or dark
I felt trapped
I froze and I did not make a sound
I didn't recognise that what was happening was sexual abuse
I didn't know that this was not normal
Feelings of humiliation washed over my body
I was embarrassed and confused
I thought I'd be expelled from school
I believed that I deserved what happened to me
What had happened didn't really hit home too hard until I was older

EVEN THE LONGEST JOURNEY STARTS WITH A SINGLE STEP

GARION POTTER

My name is Garion and I'm guessing that if you're sitting down reading this, you may have some experience in the subject of sexual abuse, be it as a survivor or a supporter. This being the case, if it's all the same to you, I'll be blunt in my words and clear in my message – sexual abuse of any kind is a blatant contempt of all existing laws of humanity and deserves only the most severe of punishments. Unfortunately, not all abuse is punished as such and I will tell you now that this is not your fault.

This is my second attempt at a story submission, with my first ending up well over 5000 words! After having read it over again, it was like a smack in the mouth – and that's not how I wanted to impart any kind of message. I am choosing to start from where I am today, work my way backwards and hopefully share with you some ways of coping or finding sunshine in the darkness, in a world that isn't such a bad place after all.

Facts: I was sexually abused as a child by a Catholic priest between the ages of twelve and nineteen. This man was also a relative of my family. Late last year my perpetrator, Father

Malum (name has been altered for legal reasons), was sentenced to six years imprisonment for four charges relating to the indecent and sexual assault of a minor, after pleading guilty in a District Court. While neither my family nor I had to testify, we were all ready if called. We weren't about to let this monster get away with what he had done. He is now sitting a jail cell, most likely in isolation for at least the next three and a half years (being his non-parole period) and I can live, knowing that he is not free.

I wanted you to read up-front about my court outcome because many rarely get the chance to see their perpetrator go to jail. To everyone who has suffered as I have and, for one reason or another, not been in a position to take on or face their perpetrator, I share this for you so we may feel as one and reclaim some of that which has been taken from us – too often in secretive violence, mistrust and silence.

In the interest of full disclosure, civil proceedings are being brought against the Roman Catholic Church of Australia for failing in their duties to provide adequate protection for vulnerable children – not for financial gain, but so they don't get away with failing the people for whom they are responsible. That being the case, I am choosing to focus on who supported me during my journey, how they did this and how I feel today about the Church and my faith, support groups, survivor advocates and dealing with trauma – while maintaining my sense of being after everything I have experienced.

Quite easily, my biggest supporter has always been my wife; I knew very early on that I had met someone special in her. After many years of being together, and with her knowledge of the relationship I had with Father Malum (who self-appointed himself as a mentor in my life where no consistent father figure was present), she challenged me mentally and emotionally by directly asking, "Were you ever abused by Father Malum?" The question caught me off guard, as I had never thought about our connection as abusive. After thinking about it for half a day, it finally struck me that I had in fact been abused for all those years!

I had been groomed since I was a child under the guise that I was being educated and shown love in an alternate way. I was told it was all to ensure that I had no hang-ups about my sexuality and that I was prepared for a relationship. My wife picked up on subtleties in my behaviour when Father Malum's name was mentioned or when I described to her the ways he told me that he cared for me. This was despite him refusing to meet or even acknowledge my wife's existence. I mean, I was confused, and I wonder what my wife must have felt at the time!

The abuse itself first started when I was twelve and continued until I was almost twenty years old. It began with subtle touching of clothing around the genital area while I was sleeping, or being asked to show him how I washed myself in the shower. The abuse eventually escalated to mutual masturbation and oral sex, all of which would mostly take place within the confines of the parish presbytery. Father Malum controlled when I hung out with friends, the types of extra-curricular activities I participated in, the types of units I studied in my HSC and my eventual career choice. To say he had an influence over me would be a severe understatement. He made me feel like I "needed" his approval and his care; he would chastise me for going against the control he subversively imparted on my everyday life and the choices I made. He would feign distaste when the news would highlight cases of historical sex abuse through institutions and made me promise that what happened between us would stay that way, as "others would not understand" what we did.

His control only ended after I met my wife, where he remarked that she was not what he had intended for me regarding a partner. He stated that while she was located remotely for university, she would be seeing other people and I was naïve for thinking that our relationship could be serious. I knew that what I had found was worth fighting for, so I did. It wasn't until my wife asked me the fateful question that I notified the police, making a statement and later being advised of Father Malum's arrest in 2016. Since 2011 I have being calling it what it really was, abuse.

I have spoken to many counsellors, psychologists, managers and team leaders, family and friends, and people who I thought were friends. All of them had varying ways of not just hearing, but actually listening to what I was saying and asking from them. They all had their own take: some chose to share it, while others chose to keep silent – either in respect for me or while simply taking the time to fully grasp and accept what had happened. Someone said to me once that I needed to be wise about whom I spoke to about the abuse, what I needed from sharing, and whether that person could give me that. That took a lot of thought and yes, I made mistakes; at times I disclosed to people I thought would be helpful and supportive to me, but simply didn't understand or have the capacity to be what I needed.

When I first disclosed to my wife and her family what had happened to me, I had no idea what I wanted to do with that information. My wife was adamant that I should report it to the local authorities, but was also very respectful that in the end it was my choice to make. After years of therapy, unboxing parts of what happened, I eventually contacted the Royal Commission Into Institutional Responses to Child Sexual Abuse. I met with a commissioner in a personal interview, made a statement towards the findings and was offered a few paths of next steps. Around this time my wife and I were scheduled to get married and I didn't want anything distracting me from being there for and with her one hundred percent, so I postponed my healing until after the wedding.

When I decided to take the mantle back up, I made

contact with a support agency recommended by the Royal Commission where I could access legal advice. I was provided with information about my options and what going down the criminal and civil litigation route may look like. While the lawyer that I contacted was wonderful, some other staff were less so. If you contact someone to seek assistance, don't be disheartened by your first experience. No one knows what you have been through; don't be afraid to be blunt in asking for what you need. Using this process, I made contact with the police to make a formal statement.

I had no idea what I wanted to get out of making a formal statement and I did not know if charging my perpetrator would help my healing. I was certainly aware that it wouldn't be easy, and it was through the support of my loved ones that I was able to take the first step in a very long and arduous process. While I don't say that to scare anyone, just be aware that in your own process, you'll meet resistance – you'll talk to people who you feel just want to get you off the phone as its nearing their lunch break. Sometimes you'll feel like you're going nowhere. Please fight with all that you have and find even one person who can lift you up when you fall.

I made a formal statement in 2016 to a truly wonderful senior detective from the Sex Crimes Squad, who throughout the process was amazing in her dedication to her investigations and to being a support to me in my capacity as both a complainant and witness.

It was decided early on that the criminal proceedings would take priority over any civil claim but choosing the right solicitor for me was a process in itself. I contacted multiple firms and had varying experiences ranging from caring and supportive, to being asked to tell my story to multiple people on the first call, including the receptionist. I eventually chose a solicitor whom I really clicked with and I felt cared about me and the harm that the Church had caused (even more so than the financial benefit of taking on my case). Don't feel rushed into making decisions about whom you work with; ask the right questions and be prepared to be knocked down more than once.

A minister of the United Church has proven to be a great friend. During one afternoon we had a discussion for almost three hours about faith, moving through an experience of sexual abuse and the criminal proceedings, while keeping my sanity intact. Believe me, this was a big step, as my faith had taken a massive hit and trusting someone affiliated with organised religion scared the living daylights out of me. Little did I know how much his advice and words would assist me when I needed them the most. He ended up being with my wife and me on the day that I was able to sit and watch my perpetrator's sentencing hearing. One of the main lessons he taught me was that if I base my worth, or the worth of the experiences I have suffered on outcomes of the "justice system", there will never be true justice for me. I needed to understand that being able to tell my story and having the people who really mattered to me listen and BELIEVE me, that was justice in itself.

If you or someone close to you has had an experience of sexual abuse, know that this is not your fault. Do not bury yourself in guilt and anguish for the choices and manipulations of another human being. You won't forget it, but it does get easier to live with. Your experience doesn't have to define you, it can be in your past, but it doesn't have to make up your present or your future. It's your journey and its personal, so don't compare it to another's if you feel like you're failing, or that you have to do one thing or another to heal. Small steps bring us closer toward a brighter future.

There is no bigger burden than the one we choose to carry alone, and I'm telling you this is NOT one of those, not now, not ever. Being a survivor of sexual abuse can be the most difficult thing you will ever experience, or not. The choice is completely up to you and there is no wrong answer.

I hope I get to meet you on your journey; my strength and my voice is lent to those that are yet to find theirs, and my love is from someone who is here to tell you that you're worth it.

Yours in kindness, love and understanding – be not afraid to hurt and feel pain, but be more than what you were yesterday and know that there is reason in your life. Godspeed.

HEALING THROUGH SHARING

ROSS

*H*ealing through sharing my story and listening to others' stories is of great importance to me. For most of my life, this was so that I could understand and make sense of my own experiences; however, I now feel sufficiently recovered that I can and want to assist others in their recovery and healing.

I live a busy and stressful work life, so for me, finding a balance is essential; I ride bicycles in an attempt to stay fit and when I have time, I ride along the coast or in the country. I have a life partner and small group of friends that are like family to me. I am well liked, and a productive team member in my place of employment. I can easily fill my evening watching documentaries, dramas, and historical shows on the television. I practice life-long learning with regards to the impact of male child sexual abuse survival. I don't have much contact with my actual family, who mostly live overseas.

For many years I had a memory of being an infant, and my mother becoming angry with me. I remember her face becoming that which as an infant I perceived as a "monster". I think that broke the formative bond that I had with her, leaving me frightened, vulnerable and feeling alone. Thus, I became the perfect subject for opportunistic paedophiles.

I can remember being sexually abused at the ages of four and seven. When I was four I was abused by an uncle. I think he volunteered to take the children home and put them to bed while my parents stayed out longer at their neighbours' place. It was around Christmas time. I also have memories of being brutally raped at the age of seven. It was by a family friend, at his home, in his boat shed, while my family were attending a small party at his house. I had been given alcohol and I was drunk.

I think I might have spoken up at the time, but I was placed in the back of a van and left to scream it out. There was no follow-up conversation about it within my family; in fact there was an unspoken rule of silence around strongly held emotional subjects. I attempted to talk to one sister about it when I was about fifty years of age, but stopped when she said she was scared about what I might say. This occurred when four of my siblings went to a celebration of our primary school's 150th year. We were in a car together and the eldest sister asked to go up a back road to visit an old family friend who was "always around" when she was growing up; this was my perpetrator.

The impact of the second episode lead me to "turn the lights off", internally at least, and the spirit of that small boy died. This was the only way I knew how to protect myself. I switched off the thing they were attracted to: a beautiful, excited, happy and connected little boy. I lived a near-mute life; I was only comfortable to speak one-on-one with a person, and never in a group. I was always afraid. This continued into my teenage years, so I was pretty alone by the time I became an adult.

In hindsight when looking back at my teenage years, I was unable to really participate in the normal sexual learnings, as I was probably terrified of experiencing sexual feelings. I had no idea why this was so at the time, as I had buried the memories as a way of surviving what had happened. Once I did become sexually active, for the majority of my life I have experienced a level of confusion about my sexuality.

I was in my early thirties when I started having memories. I had nightmares that I could not remember as well as night sweats. I had a friend who was a survivor of childhood sexual abuse, and I felt safe enough with her to bring up my concerns that I had also suffered this fate. However, throughout most of my thirties and into my forties, I did not accept these memories; I wondered whether they were an aberration of a weak person, simply making excuses, undermining my chances for success and a good life.

I wanted to understand what was happening to me, while getting to know myself better and discovering what my reality was, so I sought different forms of therapy. I found counsellors who I could work with effectively, finally finding one whom I worked with for five or six years. My counsellor was an inspiration, and together we maintained a sense of hope throughout our journey of my recovery together. During this time I completed a Bachelor of Nursing and a post-graduate qualification. I also started a new career and I enjoy this new work immensely.

A big influence has been much more recent: my participation in a male child sexual abuse survivors peer support group. The five gentlemen and two facilitators in the group reminded me of the courage required along our individual journeys. I feel that due to my recent experiences my brain wiring has changed in a healing way, and I realise that I have a role to play in society: to support survivors and work towards changing society's anxiety regarding talking about the impact of child sexual abuse.

Advice that I would like to offer young survivors of child

sexual abuse, in order to help them to maintain hope, includes the following:

- Seek support and allow yourself to be supported by others, even if you feel like you want to self-isolate because you don't understand what is happening emotionally and mentally.
- Allow yourself to grieve the loss of your innocence.
- Never, never blame yourself; always remember that you were the innocent child being taken advantage of by an adult.
- Be gentle on yourself; being self-judging and harsh on yourself plays into your perpetrator having power over you. Do not let them win.
- Learn about mental health, and how the brain works and stores information.

Also:

- Take your recovery at your own pace. It may appear to get worse for a while as you are releasing long-held, difficult memories. Give yourself the time you need to process what comes up.
- Take care with whom you divulge your child sexual abuse history. Find people you feel safe with and trust. Seek out professionals who are able to assist you in your goals.
- Find a sense of yourself that you know is your own (untainted by others), perhaps a memory of yourself before the event. Be true to that part of yourself and nurture it. Talk to him and let him grow; let this sense of self lead you in your recovery.
- Be aware that your brain has plasticity. You have your neural pathways that hold the trauma, anxiety

and distress of your abuse. But you also have millions of other neural pathways that you can utilise to build yourself a more positive sense of self and hope for your unique future.
- Learn about mindfulness and calming those distressed neural pathways. Getting out of your head and utilising the strength and resilience of your body will remind you of what you can achieve.
- For some this all may take some effort; for those who may blame their physical self for what happened to them, a healing relationship needs to occur with your body.

I would like the community to know that the perpetration of sexual abuse is always about the power of one person over another. The impact of an adult or older person doing this to a child is likely to be catastrophic to the child. As memories in young children are laid down implicitly, rather than explicitly, a child may not have clear memories and therefore not understand why they are feeling a certain way. A child's behaviour may change in response to these misunderstood feelings. A child's trust in others is likely to be greatly affected as well, leading to the creation of defence mechanisms so that the child can feel safer. It is well documented that child sexual abuse victims usually live in constant fear, or even terror – again, without perhaps knowing why. This was certainly the case in my childhood, through most of my adult life, and if I am true to myself, even somewhat today.

After being sexually abused, in which the perpetrator is usually a person known to the child, the child's ability to trust others is greatly diminished. A child needs to be allowed to rebuild this trust at their own pace. They need to (re)learn whom they can trust and decide for themselves what information to share, and to whom they are going to share this with. A child's carers need to be tolerant and respectful of this process.

Boys who are victims of childhood sexual abuse are faced with gender identity problems. Being a victim goes against our society's norms of what it is to be a man. If being a victim is sensed by other males, bullying may occur; subsequently, there is a risk of a boy becoming socially isolated, which can affect a person's mental health. In adult life, men who have been sexually abused may experience sexual confusion about their sexual preferences.

During one of the gatherings of the male child sexual abuse peer group, I stated that I feel that I am going beyond "recovery". This does not mean that I leave all of those negative experiences behind and move on. Rather, it means that I embrace all of myself, including the wounded and the "normal" parts. I utilise the knowledge that I have gained from my child sexual abuse experience in ways that better support me, others seeking assistance and the community at large. I see myself as a participant in a fellowship of similar people who are capable of listening to the heartbreak of others' experiences; and I am able to stand with them, and honour them, thus providing hope and the opportunity for healing.

WAYS OF COPING

I dissociated from an early age, disappearing into a strong fantasy world
Sport became my emotional and physical release
Anything I could to mask the emotional void
A world that allowed me to escape my reality
...some sense of escape and reassurance that things really do get better
Just keep pushing and eventually you'll turn the page and it'll all go away.
The second episode led me to "turn the lights off"
The spirit of that small boy died. The music inside him died....and so did the dance
I had nightmares, night sweats ....I kept replaying the trauma in my head
I lived trapped in a world of secrecy, guilt, and shame with thoughts of suicide and self-harm, in a childhood filled with loneliness and fear
I no longer trusted any adult figure nor liked being touched or hugged by anyone
This was the only way I knew how to protect myself
We all deal with things and cope differently

My defence was to block it out of my mind
I was always afraid, living in fear, ...pushing my problems down
I shut out my family, I blamed myself without knowing it
I withdrew and I had no interest in learning, eventually living on the streets
It was an environment in which I could not confide in anyone
I felt I was trying to stay alive on a day-to-day basis. Growing up for me was truly about survival
When I did not feel safe, I moved on
Terror, loneliness and self-inflicted isolation came from several angles
My focus was to succeed, but the higher I climbed, the emptier I felt
I pushed like an animal, a slave to my thoughts, hoping that it would all go away
I tuned the extremes of my emotions out of existence, locking my experiences away, pretending that they didn't happen
Shame told me that I was weak, that I deserved what was happening to me
Self-medicating, Self-harming....At the age of fourteen I experimented with drugs....in an attempt to block out the negative feelings.
The drugs became harder and stronger
I would wag school and get drunk with my friends. I became a social alcoholic, drinking myself into blackouts
I drove home blind drunk at 130kph with no seatbelt on, not giving a fuck if I crashed or not
I stood on the platform waiting for the next train to throw myself in front of
Being in pain made me feel insignificant
But the more I tolerated the pain, the more it actually controlled me
Pain and trauma had become a part of my identity and it dictated my life
My mental fatigue was wearing me down after years of self-blame and living in fear

I did try to tell others, I just wasn't believed, and so I internalised everything that was happening in my life

I didn't have the emotional intelligence to express how I truly felt

My faith had taken a massive hit. I found myself constantly expecting disaster to strike.

I never felt normal and I felt left behind in life

I had always doubted myself because I could not remember specific details

I avoided forming any long-term relationships with others

I buried the memories as a way of surviving what had happened

In hindsight, I recognise that it helped to see how others had and hadn't coped

I recognise how I tried to erase the beautiful boy

I became a lot quieter and withdrawn, shut down, inaccessible

I wanted to stay small, hidden, invisible. Life held no value to me

I switched off the thing they were attracted to: a beautiful, excited, happy and connected little boy

His view of love became skewed and confused. I sought to change that

Now I remind myself that I'm in control now, and I am no longer afraid to face my past

BREAKING THE TABOO

STEPHEN

In the last few years I am feeling a new lease of life as I approach what most would consider to be retirement age. I am a university professor with a successful professional life; I have received a number of awards and served on national decision-making bodies. It is the sort of career that could be taken as exemplary for those setting off on their own.

I have been married for thirty years and I have two grown-up "kids", so everything looks normal from the outside. I left home for university when I was eighteen, and left the country of my birth when I was twenty-one. I now live in Australia, the country of my dreams and I am very happy here. But lately I have had cause to wonder whether or not I was really running away.

I had an emotional crash in my early fifties that led to several years of misery, confusion, and recovery. I spent several years nursing open psychological wounds that derailed me completely from what had been my normal life. First came two years of social and professional uselessness that I managed to hide from public perception, followed by several years climbing the steep path out of the deep, bleak valley of desolation. During this time, I felt that I was practising a new identity. I would not have made it alone; my wife, boys and siblings, therapists, psychologists, social workers and fellow survivors held my hand along the way and picked me up when I stumbled. And stumble I did – several times! One of the main things this journey taught me is that in mental health, just as in physical health, you have to clean out wounds before you sew them shut.

Looking back, it is amazing I got that far in life before it happened! Now I understand so much more about my childhood, even before any sexual abuse occurred, and about the aftermath in terms of feelings, behaviour and relationships with other people in the years that followed.

I had left this all untouched – covered it up – for thirty-five years! But there comes a time when you can no longer hold it in: many survivors speak of triggers that force them to stop keeping the secrets that they have so carefully and mistakenly guarded for so many years. In my case it was a double trigger: the heftiest ever period of overwork just at the time when my own sons had reached the age that I was when I experienced the abuse. Suddenly surrounded every day by boys who reminded me of those dark years, it pushed me over the edge.

The story of abuse began with my family moving 200 km to a new area when I was thirteen. My father was required to move by his work, but my parents didn't want to. My new school was a severe culture shock in the first few weeks, as I came from a more urban environment and had been at what my religious parents perceived as the perfect school. I moved from a large co-ed semi-private school to an all-boys school in a small town where the boys seemed larger, wilder, and much more grown-up than I was used to. I felt threatened by them: boys that my mother would have kept me away from at our previous home. I had no close friends yet, so I didn't know of the dangers they knew about, and my parents organised extra evening lessons for me with a language teacher in a subject I didn't think I was weak in. They meant well; they were concerned it was a weaker school.

This man helped himself to me every week for almost a year from the very first evening onwards. Wrapped around his little finger, my parents were grateful and paid for him to abuse me for many months without knowing what they were doing. I had to either keep going back to him or tell someone what was happening – but I couldn't tell. At the time, I didn't even try to make sense of what was happening to me; this would have to wait another thirty-five years until the crash!

I unknowingly entered a period of what I now know is called hyper-vigilance; it lasted for years. It is a state of *constantly expecting* disaster to strike. Emotionally, it was like trying to swim in a round, smooth-sided tub of turbulent water being fed constantly from many taps that were fully open, and all the time I knew there was no stopper in the gurgler below, which was waiting to swallow me up and drown me. I felt I was trying to stay alive on a day-to-day basis, trying to avoid that seemingly inevitable mistake or stroke of uncontrollable destiny; it could come from any direction, throwing the miserable truth into the open and finishing me. The result is what would later be called complex PTSD, which is what I was treated for, together with depression. Now they call it complex trauma, I believe, but at the time it didn't exist yet.

Life was especially traumatic until I moved away to university five years later. Terror, loneliness and self-inflicted isolation came from several angles.

One: I was a wimpy kid – one of the smallest in the class – a late developer who shot up to normal height only from the age of 15. With this stature, I was shy, withdrawn, and had been constantly bullied at my previous schools. I must have looked an especially tasty morsel to a paedophile.

Two: it quickly became apparent to me that all the other

boys knew about this man; I didn't only because I was new at the school. So to tell anyone about *any* association with him was out of the question; I *had to* keep it secret.

Three: I was just in the process of admitting my homosexuality to myself in an environment where this alone would have made me a total outcast if it became known. There just weren't any others – there was only hostility on this subject, so here too I felt completely alone.

Four: my parents were only barely coping with the unwanted move to this area. I felt they were concentrating on themselves and on the schooling of my two elder siblings. The younger two had been "put out to graze". It was not an environment in which I could confide in anyone.

He enjoyed tormenting me with the truth only he had recognised in me. He *wanted* me to like boys and taunted me with it! He suggested names of other boys I should want, but these were only the blond ones he fancied.

He tricked me into revealing which one I most liked and then organised that all three of us be together overnight on a school trip. But when the dark boy rejected him, he outed me in a fit of rage, disclosing that we had been together for months. I was devastated and cried uncontrollably – now they would all know – but he seemed oblivious to what he had just done. He didn't care at all! I was consoled and hugged by the boy I had wanted to be hugged by, but in circumstances that couldn't be further from what I wanted! It is no wonder that these mixed messages compounded my fledgling misunderstanding of the difference between homosexuality and paedophilia, and the two became inextricably intertwined in my soul. Any reaction that was really due to the abuse, I ascribed to my homosexuality. I left home five years later convinced I had succeeded in covering up all truths, but after the crash and my recovery from it I now know I hadn't – it was just psychological self-protection soothing my ego.

The first person I told was my wife of twenty years. It was not the abuse that had prevented me from doing so earlier, but having to admit to my same-sex attractions. I had heard of so many marriages that had ended due to such revelations, and I was terrified that she would leave me. I blurted it all out in one night, but she was magnificent: she was concerned only by the abuse. Next came my siblings, and I told the story of both issues, neither of which they had known about. Telling them all of this was like continuing to throw up when your guts are long since empty – muscular spasms that have no apparent purpose – but I knew I couldn't confide in just one of them. Here again, there were only positive reactions, so part of me was left stunned and wondering why I hadn't said something sooner.

After this it got easier to talk. I went to individual therapists, initially at the insistence of my wife. At first I just needed to talk and I needed their assistance in my self-analysis of the past. I was desperate to understand what that boy went through during the years on his own, and why he withdrew from society and had always found social interactions very hard going. I felt he was still caged within me and I needed to free him and the emotions he embodied. After so many years of neglecting him, I was still objectifying him as if he were not part of me.

It sounds strange to say so, but at this stage of my recovery a new strength returned to my emotions. If you imagine your emotions can be charted like an electrocardiogram with peaks and troughs for periods of joy and sadness, it was as if the tops and bottoms of my feelings had been chopped off for years. I now recognise that my emotions had been numbed for decades: my reaction to the abuse – a coping mechanism – was that I had tuned the extremes of emotion out of existence! It was my unconscious solution to the hyper-vigilance of my teens – the only way to survive the trials of an everyday life that had psychologically tormented me so much. What a sad thing to have to realise and come to terms with after so many years – that I had killed off my emotions! This is the sort of stuff that occupied me on the road to recovery. I simply had to understand what had closed me off and how.

I also went to a group that I found especially helpful: the Survivors And Mates Support Network (SAMSN) group in Sydney was phenomenally helpful in combination with individual psychotherapy. I could talk to others who were in the same situation; each divulging secrets they had kept for too many years, but in a safe environment supported by psychologists and social workers. SAMSN runs courses in which the group discusses systematically the themes that we as survivors need to understand. It begins with analysing the family environment as a child. Every child assumes their family is normal: it is only with analysis later in life do you realise where the weaknesses lay. Later we discussed the grooming process; the emotions of shame, guilt, and anger; masculinity; the effects of abuse on later relationships; coping mechanisms, where to get help, and "how do we go on from here?"

To understand what the crash and recovery from it are like, imagine driving along a freeway built 35 years ago that you commonly use, but today there is a massive pile-up just in front of you and the road is blocked. Shaken from witnessing the accident, you have no option but to use the old road, and you drive along it remembering things as you pass them that you have not seen or thought about since your childhood. The accident is like the psychological crash: it leaves you jolted and uncertain, but therapy helps you to find and open up the old road, where there are many forgotten memories to digest. They are still in your brain, but they were inaccessible as long as the main road was open.

These things have helped me through to the point where I now consider myself essentially recovered, but as a new, reconstructed me who will never be as I was before the crash. I went through a period of existential fear that I would lose control of my life, and it took others to convince me that I had once again misidentified the source of my fear: there is no danger of abuse any more; I was only afraid of the spectre of a second emotional crash!

I am left with enormous regrets about the loss of opportunity when a teenager and in my early twenties – I call them my stolen years – but now I understand better why I stumbled into episodes of further abuse at ages when they should have been avoidable. This is where particularly the SAMSN discussions helped me lot: body language is so important and bullies and other abusers use it unconsciously to spot victims. My antennae for social norms and body language had been flattened, resulting in a kind of social disability. Several memories of my social ineptitude at the time returned and stabbed sharply into my conscience during my recovery, but now I have learned not to blame myself.

STEPHEN

Sometimes I wonder how I would cope if I were fifty years younger and the same abuse happened. Part of me thinks it must be easier now, as abuse is talked about a lot more – it just didn't exist in those days! And I could be openly gay if a teenager in Sydney today, which was unthinkable in rural England fifty years ago. But maybe these thoughts are driven by regret? The psychology of being abused and recovering from it will never be easy, and so I wonder what message I could leave for a teenager who is being or has been sexually abused today.

The most important one is: *don't wait*! You *need* to talk to people – to confide in someone – as soon as you can: that is most important! My misery was caused by my self-inflicted isolation, believing unquestioningly that telling anyone anything would result in me being an outcast. I would lose the few friends I had. But the reactions I had when I finally did divulge my secrets were mostly positive.

There is a perception – perhaps a false one, but I think common – that survivors are seen as having little chance of success in later life. This is compounded by the impression given by police dramas on TV, where criminality is almost universally attributed to neglect or abuse during childhood. It leads to an unconscious expectation – to prejudices – that these boys are condemned to lives of eternal poverty, substance misuse and gambling, and, most insidiously, should be suspects when other children are abused.

THIS IS NOT SO! The community needs to appreciate that former abused children are everywhere and in all walks of life! I am undeniably successful in my profession and other survivors are equally successful in a diversity of careers. Much of the foundation for the position of respect that I now enjoy was built in the years I described as "numb"; from society's point of view I was functioning well despite my inner turmoil. And so are many others. I fell on my nose, psychologically speaking, in the years during and after my emotional crash, but I have recovered to a point where I can work and live as effectively as before.

When childhood abuse makes the news, it is the perpetrators who are in the spotlight – the survivors are mentioned briefly, sometimes with a degree of suspicion when the perpetrator is a well-known and well-loved celebrity – and then almost immediately forgotten. There is still a taboo on talking openly about what they go through, which makes it harder for them to find help and the recovery they need.

Breaking this taboo is the next step our society needs to make.

DISCLOSING

I want all survivors to know that they will be believed and supported
Every step takes courage, and feeling safe enabled me to be honest with myself
I recognised that it was time that I begin seeing myself in the eyes of how others see me
I was in control of what I wanted to share, when, and how much
Find that one person that can hear you and help you bring down barriers
Be brave in telling others, especially your partners about your experience
Allow family and friends to see who you truly are
There is love and support around you
This support....brought out the warrior within me
I was greeted with only love, support and acceptance
I now believed I was not alone
And I was no longer going to suffer in silence
I learned to talk to others, rather than keeping things to myself
There comes a time when you can no longer hold it in
It got easier to talk, and you will be believed
I needed to be wise about whom I spoke to about the abuse
Not everyone can handle it, and not everyone knows how to respond
But know that I believe in you
You have to clean out wounds before you sew them shut
Learn what your boundaries are and stick with them
No one knows what you have been through, it's your life and journey, unique to you
And If you go down this path, be prepared to relive your story, your chronology of events, and the minute details

If you contact someone to seek assistance, don't be disheartened by your first experience if they don't handle it well

And just because someone else has a similar experience, this does not mean that your journey will be similar to theirs

Never tell someone with lived experience to "snap out of it" or "get over it" = they've got to move through it, which includes finding acceptance in their journey

Sharing your story can be a constructive process

Find people you feel safe with and trust, and don't be afraid to be blunt in asking for what you need

Tell the counsellor everything, especially about your feelings

This is strength, courage and being brave

Child sexual abuse victims usually live in constant fear, or even terror

A child or adult needs to be allowed to rebuild trust at their own pace

And connecting with other survivors has been significantly beneficial in this process

I've learnt that I am not alone, and that it is possible for me to move forward with hope and vision

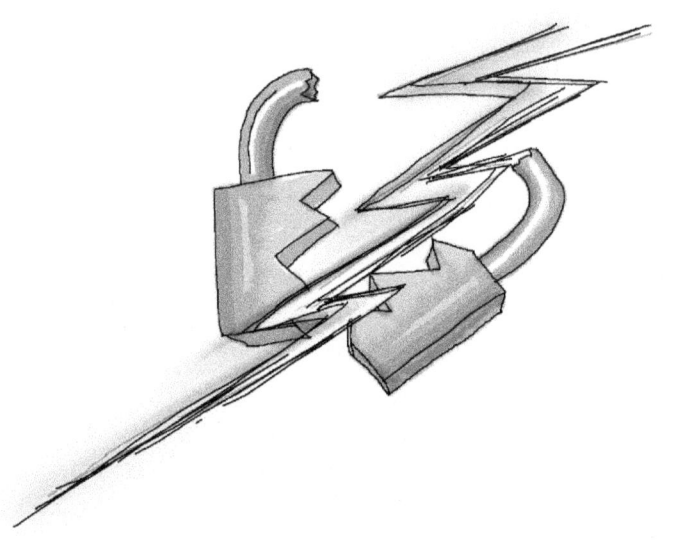

BREAKING THE STIGMA

REX

It was winter of the year 2000; I was eleven years old. As I was trying out for the Under 14 representative baseball side, I had no idea what this season would lead to. It was this winter that I was introduced to the man who would one day betray both my and my parents' trust. This was the man who would sexually assault me.

But it didn't start out as the nightmare that it would become. He, like so many other predators, was a fun and friendly guy. He would hand out soft drinks at the end of the game to all of us. He would come and attend our softball games in the off-season. He was basically a big kid in my eyes, a bit like Peter Pan: he just seemed to have never really grown up.

But looking back now, I can see it all. I see how he lured young boys like me in, gained their families' trust and then, when the time was just right, he made his move. He was clever; he picked the times, places and ways that led you to think that maybe what was happening was your fault. For me, this all unfolded in January 2004.

Over a period of six months he managed to assault me at least nine times that I can recall. At the time I knew that it was wrong, but he had convinced me that it was my fault. Being fifteen, I was also terrified about what the assault might mean for me socially. What did this mean for my sexuality? For my masculinity? What would the other kids at school say? What would my family say? These were all questions that I wasn't ready to know the answers to. At fifteen and having red hair at a public school, I already had enough to deal with.

So, I did what most male victims of male perpetrators do and I locked my experiences away, pretending that they didn't happen. I almost never thought about them. Once or twice they popped into my head but then I would tell myself that it was my problem and this was only happening to me.

This is where the deepest problem lies. It is never just you; you are not the first and you will not be the last. When he is finished with you, he will move onto someone else and until someone speaks out, there will be victim after victim.

Fast forward five years, and I am now getting married. Due to time and money constraints, my mum suggests we use an old family friend, my perpetrator, as the photographer. I did not want to raise suspicion and so I agreed. To be honest, I didn't see having him there as a big problem for me. I had put what had happened behind me. It's hard to explain, but it was a chapter in my life that I had closed. Those photos now feel tainted, just like what should be my fond memories of junior baseball.

Another five years passed and my life was going pretty well. I had a wife, two kids, I was building a house and my career was also going gangbusters. I remember that I had spent the afternoon at golf with my family and I then had a phone call. It was my mum. She didn't say much, just that she loved me and that my father wanted to ask me something. I still remember the words: my perpetrator, "… Was arrested today for sexually abusing young boys! Did anything ever happen to you? You would tell us if it did, wouldn't you?"

It was in that moment that the classic fight or flight instinct took over, and I took the flight option. I responded with, "No Dad, nothing ever happened. Of course I would tell you." We made some more small talk about the situation before the conversation ended. It was in that moment that I realised that I was not his only victim.

Later that evening, as I looked at my young daughter playing and my six-week-old son, I realised that as a parent, I had to act. If I did not have the moral courage to come forward, then how could I ever expect my children to, if they found themselves in a similar situation? I told my wife that I was going to call Crime Stoppers just to let them know that I had known my perpetrator, in case they wanted to talk to me. After reporting the incident, I still did not know how to tell my wife about the abuse. It was one thing telling a stranger and it is another telling your closest friends and family.

In the end, I antagonised her into asking me what was going on. Her reaction was not what I expected. She was hurt and betrayed, and she told me to say goodbye to our children and that I was no longer welcome in their lives. My wife told my parents, and their world shattered as well. This made me seriously question whether I had done the right thing. I seriously considered just calling the police and withdrawing my statement. The detectives were outstanding and they sent for someone across the country to meet me in person and take my statement.

This was when I found out about the anonymity. Since I was a minor at the time of the offences, I would have a closed courtroom and all names and identities would be suppressed. The only people who would have to know about the court case were the people that I told, and all of a sudden, the court case wasn't quite so scary. I realised that if I had come forward in 2004, the same situation would have applied.

For the next eighteen months, nothing really changed. I

told a few close friends from work about the case and the Department of Public Prosecutions (DPP) kept me informed about the progress of the case. In late 2015, a colleague of mine took his own life, and I wondered if I could be doing more with my own life. It was around this time that the DPP had informed me that my perpetrator was pleading guilty, which meant that I did not need to attend court as a witness. However, they would still like me to consider providing a Victim impact statement (VIS).

VISes are actually incredibly powerful, as they are the victim's chance to describe the lasting effects that the trauma has had on them. At first, I didn't know what to write, but once I started, it all just flowed out. It was at this time that I made the decision to speak publicly about my experiences. As a young person, I wanted to hear and see victims sharing their stories, not just read about them. In the male victims' arena, there was only one man that I could find who had shared his story.

The DPP were extremely supportive and they arranged for me to read my VIS in court. Of the eight victims, I was the only one to provide a statement and to read it aloud. I felt like I was finally telling my perpetrator what I thought of him; even though it was too late to make a difference in our lives, he would now have to answer for his crimes that his victims, like me, have to live with. I was scheduled to speak to a reporter outside the court afterwards, but I felt that I owed it to my family to tell them the outcome first. Mum and Dad already knew, but the rest of my family didn't.

The hardest phone call I have ever made (and that I think I will ever make in my life) was to my grandparents. I didn't know how to explain to them what had happened and I just didn't think that I could ever look them in the eye again. All of a sudden, I was feeling doubt and I wondered what my friends and colleagues would say when they saw me on the news. Thankfully I went ahead with the interview; afterwards, I was inundated with emails and Facebook posts of support. The biggest impact on me at that time was when a friend reached out and told me that he too was a victim, and that seeing me speak out gave him hope and strength for his own recovery.

Suddenly I had arrived at where I wanted to be. Not because I was a public figure, but because I was making amends for my adolescent years. I became involved in radio interviews, newspaper articles and a number of TV appearances. Each time I spoke out publicly, someone new would reach out to me to share their experiences. The most powerful of these came earlier this year, when a man called up the radio station in tears and said that he was a victim in 1973 and had never told anyone. Through hearing me speak, he had realised that his time to speak was now. I was blown away, speechless and in tears myself.

I am not normally an emotional person, but hearing this man's words felt so powerful. When I think that I had ever considered withdrawing my statement, this now just seems so absurd. This is my job now, this is my purpose: to bring men of all ages out of the shadows and to break down the stigma surrounding male victims of sexual abuse.

Although for me it might seem like it's too late, the impact that I am making through helping other men is no longer too little.

RECOVERING

My life started again when I made that phone call
That conversation with my friend was the turning point
I experienced strong feelings of fear and anxiety
My eyes could not unsee what they had seen
And I clung to the glimpse of pure love from the other side
I was tired of disappointing myself
Reminiscent to my own sense of failure as a son, it presented in my role as a parent
I had so much unresolved grief that I didn't realise I was carrying
But I knew that what I had found was worth fighting for
I maintained some hope
There and then, I committed to myself that I would do whatever it took to become a better man.
I began to have trust in my life, and I was no longer the victim
I was going to face everything, even myself
It was an emotional rollercoaster to relive those past events throughout the investigation and trial
I am glad that I have started to work through it
I again found my passion in music
I recognise now that there was a part of me seeking help to heal which was bigger than the dark and broken part of me
This little truth started to ripple out and create changes across my life
A great anger grew in me
While I can never undo what has occurred, I can turn my anger into action to fight injustice
While the effects of the abuse will always be with you, it can grow to be like a comet, only appearing briefly with long periods out in the cosmos where it is not affecting you.

I also know that I am now strong and resilient enough to no longer run away form my past and I can tackle it head on
I'm still evolving with emotional triggers and wounds
But I am stronger now than I've ever been
I've come to learn that the trauma does not define who I am
I want to continue to find happiness in my life
And to speak from a place of joy rather than suffering and anger
I know that I'm not responsible for other's actions
I am safe now. I am a survivor, and I am proud of that
I am proud of what I have in life
The path to happiness for me was in emotional healing
The demons I faced could not compete with the light of love
I still saw light. I still felt loved
So take your recovery at your own pace, it's an individual process, it cannot be measure against any other person's recovery

RUNNING FREE

DAVID NGUYEN

I'm a thirty-eight year old husband, father of three amazing children and a child protection worker. I'm also a survivor of child sexual assault.

After twenty-nine years of being silent, I made the very tough decision to go public with my story in 2018. With the support of my amazing wife who I have been with for eighteen years, we made the decision together to go public in the hope that this inspires other survivors to know that they can heal, and most importantly, to give our children a voice. My wife from day one of our relationship has accepted me for who I am and made me believe that I could achieve anything that I wanted to achieve. She has provided me with unconditional love and has given me hope when I thought that this was lost because of my past.

While growing up, my mum was and is the most amazing, supportive and loving mother. I came from a good family and I wouldn't fit the stereotype of a child "at risk". My abuser was a close family friend who groomed my parents and me for a couple of years before any abuse took place. He sexually assaulted me on four separate occasions over a twelve-month period.

Telling my mother about my abuse was one of the hardest conversations I have ever had and this only occurred in April last year. To be honest, I had no idea how my mother would react. "Was she gonna believe me, was she gonna blame me for what happened? Should I really tell her when the research shows that one in three adults don't believe kids when they disclose?" What a shocking statistic this in itself is.

Being the amazing mother that my mum is, I was greeted with only love, support and acceptance. It's a moment that I will never forget, when Mum and I just hugged each other and she told me how much she loved me and how proud of me she was.

Since sharing my story, I know that some people's first reaction would have been, "Where were his parents and how did they not know what was going on?" My abuser was a trusted family friend whom we had known for years. I reassured my mum that at no point did I ever blame her for what happened, nor will I ever. The only person who should be blamed is the perpetrator, not anybody else.

I believe that every child has the right to feel safe, confident and free from the terrible consequences of child sexual assault. At the age of eight years old, I lost that and my childhood innocence was violently taken away from me. I lived trapped in a world of secrecy, guilt and shame with thoughts of suicide and self-harm, in a childhood filled with loneliness and fear.

I remember after being abused, I no longer trusted any adult figure or liked being touched or hugged by anyone. I would run away from anyone who would try to give me a hug, or I would freeze and sit there, expecting them to sexually assault me. At the age of fourteen I experimented with drugs, taking excessive ecstasy, speed and acid in an attempt to block out the negative feelings.

So why did I hold onto my pain for so long and why couldn't I simply just get over it? Being in pain made me feel significant. It gave me a role and an excuse for when I stuffed up or failed. My story made me feel unique and special; through holding onto it, it gave me a way to control my emotions. Even when it was a negative emotion. I could feel pain when I wanted to – it felt like it was a controlled pain. However, the more I tolerated the pain, the more it actually controlled me and the more that the pain held power. Pain and trauma had become a part of my identity and it dictated my life. I kept replaying the trauma in my head, until NO MORE.

I've had a lot of knockbacks in facing my inner demons; however, this doesn't mean that I have to stay down. I have learned that it's okay to fail at times, because it simply means that I have given it a go and I am taking steps in my recovery and healing. If I hadn't taken those steps, it would mean that I hadn't lived.

Know that hitting rock bottom becomes a good foundation to build and grow from. And you will fail from time to time – know that that's okay. Just make sure that you keep growing, keep standing, keep moving forward, and keep taking that extra step. If you see someone who is down, pick them up along the way.

Running has been very healing for me. Despite this, there is not a run that goes by where I don't have a flashback about my abuse. The difference now is that I'm in control of how I react and respond. I choose whether or not I'm going to replay the abuse in my head over and over again or not. I am a completely different person to when I was abused and I choose to no longer continue to blame myself for my abuse. I choose to no longer be ashamed of my abuse. I choose to live in the moment and to be thankful for the life that I have now and for the people who are in my life. I appreciate each day, choosing to live with purpose and happiness, and using this as my way to demonstrate resilience and strength. Through this, I can choose to no longer allow my trauma experiences to define me. This is strength, courage and being brave. And ultimately, your opinion of yourself is all that matters.

I've made it my life's work to overcome my experiences and I have found my purpose in life: to be here in this moment. All of the pain and suffering that I have experienced is for this. My purpose is to lead by example and to show my scars, so that people know that they can heal and create happy and amazing memories in their lives. It is one thing to overcome something, and it is another to then be able to speak about it from a place of joy rather than suffering and anger. When we can do this, we are able to find peace for ourselves.

Here I would like to share a piece that I wrote which explains the role that running has had in my recovery. (Long post disclaimer.)

Oh man that was a hard run to complete this morning. It was my hardest one yet, both physically and mentally. It was cold, windy and raining pretty hard and at the 17km mark, it was paltering down and I was already drenched. As the run got harder I actually said to myself WTF am I doing here? Is it really all worth being out here? Self doubt started to kick in, so I started heading back home.

At this point, it was like BOOM! I experienced a flashback, however this wasn't the normal kind of flashback that I would usually get. This flashback brought me back to the exact moment where I was first abused. I could see his cream door opening. I could see the colour of his bed sheets. I could see the patterns on his pillow cover. I could even smell his strong cologne.

As I ran around the last corner to arrive home, I saw a reflection of me in a window and I just stood still, crying my eyes out. I told myself that I had two options, to go home and just brush that flashback away like I usually would, or to turn around and push to run the 30km's and to process my flashback.

Fuck it...I reminded myself that I'm in control now and that I am no longer afraid to face my past. And so I turned around and recommenced running.

To be honest, life was much easier when I wasn't having to process my past and I could have easily continued life, pretending that I was ok. If I did this, I would have been hiding from the truth and running away from the fact that deep down I was broken and never at peace with my abuse. I knew that I would never find peace if I didn't overcome my experiences.

I had to figure out how to manage my suffering and my past, as it was something that would always be a part of me. I knew that if I faced my truth and got through my shit mentally, I would be able to face anything else that life threw at me. In facing my truth, it also meant that I had to suffer. I knew that I had to suffer to experience growth, but I also knew that on the other side of suffering, I would experience greatness.

My mental fatigue was wearing me down after years of self-blame and living in fear. Through the burden of carrying my secret and worrying about how other people may view me, I felt worn down. The mind is a powerful thing. It knows what your weaknesses are, it knows your fears, it guides you to places that you don't want visit. So already the mind had won and it will always win until you reprogram it. I had to reprogram my mind.

I am blessed to have my wife in my life who supports and challenges me every day. She reminded me of why I decided to take this crazy journey and participate in the 777 running events. After chatting to my wife, I realised that by me doing the 777s, I wasn't just training for a race. I haven't been getting myself out of bed at 3.30am rain, hail or shine to simply train myself to run 295kms in 7 consecutive days in 7 states. I realised that this was training for life.

I was training for when life gets hard, so that I can reprogram my mind to be positive. I was showing my mind that no matter how hard my life has been, no matter how much my childhood sucked, I am still strong, I'm still standing and I will never be broken.

I knew that at some point during the week of the 777s, I would hit my rock bottom, especially when I was physically and mentally fatigued. If I were to be honest, I was shit scared about running but I also know that I am now strong and resilient enough to no longer run away from my past and I can tackle it head on.

For those reading this, remember that your greatest strength will be found in your weakest moments. And every step takes courage, and every step saves a child. It is my hope that other survivors understand that our past will always be with us and it will never go away. But it no longer defines us and you can take control back. And on the days when you can't, it's ok but when you are down, make sure that you reach out and ask for help. There will be so many people that are willing to support you and get you through. Remember that we are NEVER alone.

One of my biggest learnings this year, and one of the hardest to implement is my wife constantly telling me that it is time that I begin seeing myself in the eyes how others see me. I promise that I am starting to see myself in this light.

For twenty-nine years I lived in silence about my past, worried about how people would perceive me as a result of low self esteem. I was living alone and I felt ashamed of my past. Running the 777's changed all of that due to me having so much support around me. It was this support that brought out the warrior within.

To my eight year old self, I would like to say that I'm proud of you for your strength, courage and resilience. Know that your past was never your fault and that you will overcome this and go on to create amazing memories. Don't ever stop fighting and don't ever lose hope. You are always worthy and strong, and you always will be.

To my fellow survivors, I want you to know that I truly love you and know that you are never alone. Your past does not define you. Sometimes people with the worse history end up creating the best futures. We each have the power to choose to create our own story.

Lastly to the guy that abused me, I forgive you. It doesn't matter anymore what you did to me, you couldn't destroy me. I'm still standing, I'm still strong and I always will be.

Another Breakthrough Moment

I recently had a breakthrough moment about regaining control in my life and I wanted to share this with everyone.

Since starting my new role I have found myself feeling mentally tired. The content that I'm expected to deliver triggers my past. It's triggered my wounded adult and to be honest, the survivor in me is sick of fighting. He has fought for thirty-two years every day.

We are often our biggest critics but mine stems from being sexually abused as a child. For most of my life, I blamed myself for my abuse and every time I failed at something I would often say to myself that I was never good and worthy enough to be happy and succeed in life.

I recently realised that despite all that I have achieved in life, I hadn't done it for myself. I did it to prove to my abuser that I was strong, happy, worthy and my pursuit for happiness was to get back at my abuser.

I was recently chatting to a friend and they asked me to think about a statement. That statement was "I don't need to prove myself to my abuser anymore". I realised that my abuser and past still controlled the person that I wanted to be and become.

Everything that I have achieved in life thus far is because I have worked hard for it and never given up on my goals...I've been resilient and despite my critic and victim always trying to bring me down, I have become more resilient and I have always faced my fears head on.

My new motto for life is "I control my life, and I control my happiness", because I don't need to prove myself to my abuser anymore. I know I'm strong, I know I'm worthy, I know I'm loved and my abuse was never my fault.

I can decide who I want to be and I will!!!

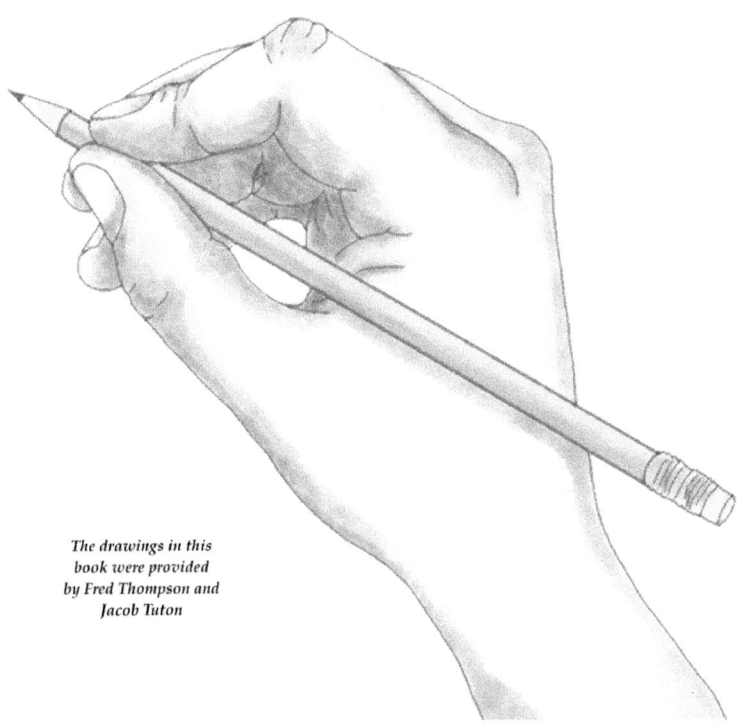

The drawings in this book were provided by Fred Thompson and Jacob Tuton

HOW DARKNESS BECAME MY BRIGHT LIGHT

MARK COOPER

As an eight-to-twelve year old boy, the days should have been filled with playing outside, riding my bike with friends and generally running amuck, not having any cares about the challenges life had for me. Instead, worrying about how am I being judged, and how people may see or think about me, filled some of the dark times of my childhood. *Lonely*, *self-conscious* and *introverted* would be how I described my childhood.

I was unable to avoid sexual predators while walking through life – this was difficult for me, as I felt they were surrounding me. Brothers, neighbours and even a family friend made it feel difficult for me to avoid these predators. Was I the one leading them on? Was I the one sending them signals? Or was I enjoying what was happening? These were not questions that a child should be thinking about; after all, I was just an innocent child.

Like many survivors of child sexual abuse, I too certainly felt dirty and violated. I experienced low self-esteem but most of all, I felt a sense of loneliness. As a child, I didn't really have a good grasp of the difference between right and wrong, but I knew what was occurring was clearly wrong, as it was always a secret and the abuse occurred when no one else was around.

The real healing started the moment that I was informed and I truly started to believe that I wasn't the one responsible for any of the abuse that happened to me. I wasn't the one causing the abuse. These questions were confirmed during a conversation I had with a friend. We weren't real close as friends back then, but he made me feel very comfortable, allowing me to drop my barriers a little as we shared our stories with each other. This has grown into an amazing friendship. Just when I felt the world was against me, I had found a dear friend walking with me.

If I was able to measure the material of these barriers that I held up to protect myself, they were as tough as any brick wall. I felt that there was nothing that would enable me to lower them. I was going to go through life with this secret and share it with no one – well, so I thought. This conversation with my friend empowered me and was definitely the turning point that would start the move from my dark place to seeing a flash of light ahead. That is the path I need to walk down now – and I had someone walking alongside me.

Surrounding myself with good and positive people who validated my existence, allowing me to speak openly, has enabled me to heal. Later in life, there was a sense that a part of me was seeking help to heal, bigger than the part of me that was dark and broken.

This healing started from around the age of thirty-five. Sharing my "story" with some other close friends in whom I trusted was the next stage when I was able to see the light ahead brightening up. I now began to have trust in my life and my barriers were definitely lowering.

Telling Mum when I was about thirty-five was by far the most difficult thing I have ever had to do. Not only was I informing Mum that I was sexually abused as a child, if that wasn't hard enough for her to hear, I was actually abused by four men, all whom she knew and trusted me with. More painful for her to hear was that two of the abusers were my two older brothers. It was devastating to see her face, listening to my story, but I knew that she needed to hear it and I needed to be the one to tell her. I held Mum in my arms as she cried and said that she had failed me as a mother. She was meant to be there to protect me and she failed at that.

After the death of my mother, I felt that I owed her some closure, which saw me go to the police to share my story. This was more about the story of my eldest brother, who was definitely a predator and I was far too often his prey. It was explained to me that the legal procedure was a long and drawn-out process, which it certainly was. After three visits to make an official statement at the local police station with SOCIT (Sexual Offences and Child Abuse Investigation Team), it was all too much for me to pursue, given where I was in my healing process.

At this stage in my life, I had started to share my story with some friends and my mother. I now believed that I was not alone. I was no longer afraid of what had happened, nor was I ashamed. I was no longer going to suffer in silence; I was a survivor and I was proud of that. I also knew that these actions were not my fault. I had suffered in silence for so long, ashamed and disgusted, yet I knew that the only way that I would be able to get answers to the questions of "why" and to take some power back was to confront one of my perpetrators.

I wrote a letter to one of my perpetrators, as I felt that this would help me. The abuse from him was different to any of the others and I didn't feel that his abuse was like a predator against his prey. Here, there was more of a feeling of love and affection – of course, remembering that I was about twelve at the time. It is fair to say that I was still a minor and he was in his late teens, and should have known better. My letter to him allowed me to acknowledge that I was aware of what he had done to me but more importantly, I had forgiven him for what he did.

Getting an extremely honest reply from my perpetrator was both exciting and empowering for me. He was able to share with me how he had remembered everything that had happened and apologised for it. My questions were answered honestly, sharing that he had been in a part of his life where he was craving something that was missing for him; affection. I was able to give him affection. I have been able to speak to him since receiving his reply and we have caught up on numerous occasions, where we have openly shared about what happened between us. This by no means trivialises the abuse, but it has reassured me to continue walking further towards the brighter days of my life ahead. I was no longer the victim of child sexual abuse; I was a survivor and I had many good days ahead.

I never wanted to be a victim. My drive was to be the victor and not allow this story to shape me as a person. To not use "I was abused" as an excuse in my life choices.

When I was around forty, I decided that it was time that I sought help from a professional and I was referred to local sexual abuse counselling services. Never did I feel that I needed professional help, but I was quickly proven wrong. I had so much unresolved grief that I didn't realise I was carrying. I knew that I was a survivor and I thought that I was in a good space mentally. Sitting face-to-face and tapping in further into my life flattened all of my barriers. As a typical male, somewhat stubborn and thinking "I'm fine" was not entirely accurate. I had lost parts of my life and needed to gain more answers.

I was referred to some group support sessions through the centre. I was able to openly share my experiences and listen to other stories too. These sessions were challenging but very rewarding – it helped to see how others had and hadn't coped with different situations. This demonstrated to me that we all deal with things and cope differently. I felt that I had in fact coped extremely well. I never turned to alcohol or drugs, and I never had self-harm or suicidal thoughts, which seemed to be a common experience of survivors of child abuse within the group.

Yes, we all cope differently and we all have some coping strategies that may or may not work for everyone. There have been three strategies that have worked for me and allowed me to see that there is a bright light ahead.

THE FIRST IS to ensure that you find that one person that can hear you and help you bring down some barriers you have up to protect yourself from any more harm or hurt in your life. In my experience, I knew that I was being heard and definitely not judged. I felt safe and this enabled me to be honest with myself.

I now know that if you stay silent, the darkness won't get any brighter. I was able to get to a stage where I was comfortable sharing my story with family and other friends. Not having someone to share with would have kept me in a dark place and may have later led to some physical or psychological harm. Allow family and friends to see who you truly are, which can be difficult in itself – but if you have secrets, then you won't ever be able to reclaim your power.

As a male, I believed that seeking professional help was a sign of weakness. Yet, professionals have been trained to understand feelings and emotions, and to also guide me to seek answers to those questions that have gone unanswered – and to shape a more positive future for myself.

These are some of the challenges of life, and no challenge is greater than being a survivor of child sexual abuse, but I have grown to be very resilient because of the coping strategies I have shared.

PERPETRATOR

My abuser was a close family friend who groomed my parents and me
He became part of my family at a time when
I was somehow an outsider within my own family
The trust afforded him was so great....
He was my hero and I idolised him
I see now that he held all the power
It didn't start out as the nightmare that it would become
I had been groomed since I was a child, I know now that I was not his only victim
And I see how he lured young boys like me, the shy, withdrawn, and constantly bullied
He had an influence over me, he gained my trust and the trust of my parents
He could behave and act how he liked, and I was at his mercy
A part of me knew that it was wrong, but he had convinced me that it was my fault
All he wore was underpants
And when the time was just right, he made his move
It began with seemingly innocent touching....and then eventually, full-on rape
What began as harmless wrestling quickly turned into a complete violation of my body
And thinking about him now makes me feel anxious, tight in my chest, sick in my stomach
I hated my perpetrator even more for what he had done to me and the power he still held over me
I was such easy prey – a needy kid with an absent father
I must have looked an especially tasty morsel to a paedophile
Parts of the attack itself are vivid and detailed, there are still gaps

*It was always a secret, and when no one else was around
Later, I would try to make eye contact with him with hatred in my eyes
It doesn't matter anymore what you did to me, you couldn't destroy me*

KEEPING GOING

TIM ROSE

It's late afternoon on a cool, yet sunny suburban winter's day, sitting on my front verandah with yet another mug of hot tea, listening to my magpies warble before their afternoon feed. They're simple pleasures in a not-so-simple world or life. I'm actually sitting here thinking about getting a tattoo, a semicolon. As a tattoo, they are a symbolic message of hope and solidarity, or affirmation against suicide or depression. It is an acknowledgement that the story continues. I don't have any tattoos, and I've felt a little scared about it to be honest.

Right now I'm a married dad of forty-five years of age, a current Masters student, counsellor, art therapist, and a Lego enthusiast. I love music, cinema, architecture, photography, art, and I feel right at home in my kitchen preparing food for friends and family – it really is the heart of my home. But back then? Back then it was a different story.

I'm a survivor of childhood sexual abuse. I was twenty-six when I first came to recognise that I had been sexually abused. I had my suspicions, but it wasn't until talking with a friend one night, and he disclosed that he'd been sexually abused, that I came to understand that what I had experienced was sexual abuse too.

My abuse began before the age of four and lasted until adulthood. I grew up in a paedophile ring in the suburbs of the east coast of Australia, of which some neighbours were a part. Some of these perpetrators, all men, were known to me, and others were not. I didn't recognise that what was happening was sexual abuse. I didn't know that this was not normal. There were particular people's homes where I would spend the night sometimes, where there was lots of nudity and sexual behaviour, pornographic pictures on the walls, and where I always had nightmares. I grew accustomed to different things being done to me. So desperate for the love, touch and attention that I wanted and needed, and wasn't getting at home, I was such easy prey – a needy kid with an absent father. And I was young. This made me popular, and while I didn't like everything that was done to me, I was being touched and I felt like someone cared for me and loved me.

When I was older, some of these things felt amazing and made me feel good, if only temporarily. It wasn't long before I'd feel such horrible guilt and dirtiness. Often, I wanted to experience the amazing feelings again, but at the same time there were other things which hurt a lot, and I was taught to "take it like a man". I was meant to be quiet or show that I really liked what was being done to me, that I wanted it. It made me feel really confused sometimes. As an adult, the idea of "taking it like a man" held a much stronger meaning, not just quietly enduring the pain that was being inflicted upon me (most often oral or anal penetration by an adult man much bigger than me). It was confusing to me to experience these feelings when I didn't want what was happening, especially leading up to and during adolescence. "Why would my body respond like that when I wanted to run away, or it hurt? What is this 'stuff' coming out of my penis?"

I felt a lot of confusion at times about what sex was, but also about attraction and arousal. Adolescence brought with it a whole range of different feelings and sensations, which were often in conflict with one another. There were times where I wanted to die, wrestling with how I could take my own life, while at the same time hearing the family rhetoric that suicide is the coward's way out. I couldn't talk to anyone about what I was feeling or experiencing. I did want to die. I wanted it all to be over. There was a loud and familiar voice in my head that I came to know as shame. Shame told me that I was weak, that I deserved what was happening to me, that I was disgusting, and that I didn't make the grade.

I felt strong pressure to be just like the other boys. This meant being tough and unemotional, being into sports and cars, perving on girls, having sex with girls – and the bigger your genitals, the more of a man you were. I was none of these things. I was creative, tactile and emotional, I loathed sports, I was sexually active with males and not well endowed physically. In fact, my earliest memory of abuse involved me being shamed by two adult men who mocked me and made fun of the size of my penis. I can still see this image in my mind. This shaming, the belief that was instilled in me that I didn't measure up, and later that I was not man enough, impacted me deeply and has affected me through my whole life.

As men, I believe that we want to fit in, to be included, but we judge one another, having created a hierarchy of standards against which one is more or less of a man. Against these standards, I was always lesser.

I wrestled with my sexuality for years, not sure if I was gay or straight. When I was sixteen, a female employer (one of two women to abuse me) began grooming me, and eventually abused me. She provided me with pornography and condoms at work, even encouraging me to go and masturbate during work hours. In hindsight, I feel that her efforts were to "convert me" to being straight by showing me what sex with a woman was like, and how good it is. I remember instances of having gone home and trying to scrub myself clean in the shower, scrubbing and scratching at my skin until it was red and inflamed, trying to wash off their smell, the feeling of them on my skin, or their fluids on different parts of my body. I remember lying on the floor of the shower crying from pain or how bad I felt about myself, how dirty and disgusting I felt.

Years later, in my thirties, I began accessing a service for adult survivors of childhood sexual abuse. I wasn't exactly like everyone else there, but for the first time in my life, I was part of a group where we all had that one thing in common, and we all knew that it was the worst thing we had experienced or been subjected to in life – we were all equal. Yes, I think we tried to measure one another up and employ some stupid hierarchy, but it didn't work. In the end it didn't matter. What did matter was us: our journeys and experiences, the lives we would have preferred to live, how we want to be different, and how we fought what the abuse told us, taught us and conditioned us to be. That became the lifesaver. It was where I found ways to resist the abuse, to see what I had done in my life and not be held prisoner by it, and to resist the effects of the abuse and find ways to begin to live my preferred life. This was my first experience of feeling that I was okay the way I was.

There were times when I questioned the existence of God or a higher power, and especially why "they" didn't do anything about what I was being subjected to. And I don't know the answer. I do know, however, that I didn't die. I wasn't overdosed and I've been able to build a life. It hasn't been easy, but I am, essentially, okay.

It's not often plain sailing. I have spent a long time in counselling and with the aid of medication to get to where I am today. It's not over yet, of course, but I'm much further from where I started. There are bad days, weeks, months and years, but years are less frequent, and the months, weeks and days are less intense in their severity.

I became a parent in my thirties, and despite wanting to be a parent for most of my life, I had no idea of what I was in for. Harder still was the reality that I was in no way prepared for the challenges I would experience because of the abuse I'd been subjected to as a child and adolescent. There was a part of me that was so scared of becoming a parent. I felt that I wasn't enough as a man, and so how would I show my children what it is to be a man? And what if I had a son – would I be able to relate to him at all? Could we be equals? Would he respect me and see me as a good example of a man? And what about that dreaded idea about victims of abuse becoming abusers? As horrible an idea as that is (and I feel nauseated even typing those words), it is sadly a common fear which many male survivors of sexual abuse experience. We worry that we might turn out like "them", whoever it was who subjected us to abuse.

Parenting really is a massive role. I've worked to be the best parent that I can be, and not having had good examples growing up, it's been hard work to parent differently than the way I was parented. I have sought to allow space for the expression of feelings and individual personhood, to listen well, to value input and to seek collaborative engagement about how and why we do things as a family. I have also tried to instil a good understanding of consent and autonomy over one's body, and to generate an open family culture which allows approachability, space and time for talking about difficult and personal things.

My family suspected that I was being abused, even to the point of collecting photographic evidence. Years later, while in therapy, I asked about what they had done regarding their suspicions, and what action they had taken to protect, support and care for me. It was distressing to learn that they had opted to do nothing since I hadn't told them it was happening, and as there was no confirmation, they therefore took no action. I've struggled with this in many ways. To me, it affirms this idea that I was responsible for disclosing what I could not make any sense of at all. This only served to re-affirm unhelpful ideas that no one would believe me, that I didn't matter, and that deep down I wanted this to happen to me.

Most significant was the idea that I was responsible for my own wellbeing. This lack of action had a very significant impact upon me, causing me to feel that I was simply not worth enough, which only served to reinforce how badly I felt about myself. There are still days that this sense of feeling bad is loud within my head. It's taken a lot of therapy, counselling and personal work to get to where I am today, and to try to counter those voices and ideas that tell me I'm shit as a person.

I've been fortunate to have a caring partner journey with me through all of this, and her family has been an immense support to me. Sadly, my own family has not done well to support or care for me amid this. I have also found that connecting with other survivors has been significantly beneficial, even to simply know that I am not alone, but more so to know that we are affected in similar and differing ways: that we are impacted and our lives and families are impacted; that there are preferred and non-preferred ways of being; and that we are alive, able to tell our stories. Perhaps we can even be for ourselves what others were not, or were unable to be for us.

I can hold and honour the little boy inside of me who is trying to make sense of the nonsensical. I can see and recognise the ocean of feelings and confusion that he feels because of (and as a result of) what he has been through. I can tell him that I believe him; I hear and believe his truth. I can show him that I am prepared to – and will, in fact – stand up for him. And I can tell him that I love him. This goes far beyond that little boy. It affects the kind of person that I am: the kind of friend, father, partner, ally, counsellor and community member I am – it literally feels like everywhere.

In many ways, this has been a process of unlearning, but at the same time it has been about learning how to express my feelings: saying "no" or "yes", voicing my needs and desires, exploring my sexuality to understand what I do and do not like doing (or have done to me), and being able to assert who I am as a person. It has also been a journey of learning who I am underneath all of the crap of my own experiences and having been violated, and being able to be that person as fully and freely as I am able to be.

And I am fortunate too that despite all of this, I am a leader among men. I work as part of a men's movement with the purpose of helping men to more fully and functionally live as who they are and address the dysfunction, difficulty and/or disadvantage in their lives. Despite decades of feeling that I have never measured up or met the grade in what it means to be a man, I am showing other men what it means for me to live as authentically as possible, while supporting them to do the same.

What does hope look like? Well, part of it is continuing to do the work that I need to in order for me to be as free and fully myself as possible. It's also working with others, especially men, and helping them to be more fully and authentically who they are. It's sharing my story, as I'm doing here, with other survivors and those who want support. A significant factor too, is in identifying as a survivor rather than as a victim. I understand that in legal terms, I am a victim, but seeing myself as a victim creates a prison that keeps me trapped in certain ways of thinking and feeling – the perpetrators still win. Recognising myself as a survivor, on the other hand – knowing that I'm still here and able to tell my story, and that I am far more than what I have been subjected to, or what I have experienced – allows me to be more, and to continue to further free myself from what I was subjected to.

What I've shared here is really just the tip of the iceberg – there really are so many layers to all of this, and there's only so much I can include here. One-on-one and group counselling and psychological support have been highly beneficial for me, and I can recommend connecting safely in a group with other good men, in the ways that you are able. There are support groups run by organisations where it is possible to connect with other survivors. I know from experience that this is hard – I've been there, and honestly, it wasn't easy (it still isn't at times), but it is well worth it.

You might be reading this because you are a survivor yourself. If that is the case, I'm so sorry that you've been subjected to abuse. Please know that you are not alone, and that you are far more than what you see or feel about yourself, what the abuse itself tells you, or what perpetrators have conditioned you to believe. You are incredible. You might be into sports and cars, and that's okay. You might love chick flicks, be sensitive and like to dance, and that's okay. You might feel scared to death about sex or sexuality and not have any idea where to go or how you could share your life with another person – that's perfectly okay too. However you are as a man is okay.

If you're reading this as someone working to support someone else that you love or care about, thank you so much for taking the time to read this book. I'm hopeful that through me (as well as the other men here) sharing my story, it has helped you to see how deeply sexual abuse can affect a person, and what you might be able to do to support those you care about. We need and are often indebted to people like you!

KEEPING GOING

Whoever you are, and for whatever reason you're reading this, please keep going and keep doing what you're doing to be the best you that you can be, and thanks for reading. As for me, this mug is empty, and it's time to head inside and put the kettle on again.

THE RIPPLE EFFECT

KEVIN WHITLEY

My name is Kevin and I'm a survivor of childhood sexual abuse, or CSA. I'd like to speak to you about hope, and how seemingly small actions can create a ripple effect that brings about change and can provide a voice to all of the silent victims out there.

Victims are groomed to remain silent. As children we're told by the perpetrator that this is to be kept secret with veiled (and often not so veiled) threats. We're told that we'd get into trouble from the police or our parents – or there are even threats made of violence against our loved ones. Often special treats or favours would be withdrawn if The Secret were ever revealed. We suffer shame, humiliation, embarrassment, anxiety and feelings of inadequacy. This ripples through our life and into adulthood. To cope, we often lock away those dreadful memories of the past into the deep, dark oceans of our mind. Our voices are taken away.

I want every victim of CSA to have a voice and know that they CAN make a difference. Not only to expose the perpetrators and the scourge of CSA, but most importantly, for themselves to take back the power and energy that these vampires stole from them as children.

The Royal Commission investigated cases of sexual abuse in the entertainment industry. We all followed the high-profile cases. My story falls within this category.

My sexual abuse experience started in the early 60s when I was just a little boy of eight years old. My perpetrator is now in his seventies and throughout his life he owned and operated several theatres. He ran these theatres utilising children and teenagers as his staff, and made a small fortune off their backs.

He produced numerous pantomimes which were all cast by children. These pantomimes were run during school holidays, so he surrounded himself with plenty of fodder from which he could choose and groom his victims. I first met him when I was about eight years old and I began working for him. He was about nineteen at the time – an adult in my eyes, yet soooo very different to my parents. He was funny, zany, irreverent, and loved chocolates and ice creams and sweets, just like a kid. He was also generous in sharing these with me. To a kid, this was like Christmas because my mum and dad wouldn't allow me to have these treats, nor could they afford them. Better still, he owned a theatre! So, wooooooooow! It really didn't get much better than this for a young boy!

As we've all come to learn in life, there is no such thing as a free lunch and this man's generosity was no exception! This was his modus operandi and this is how the grooming started. He gained my trust and the trust of my parents by providing me with the perceived kudos among my peers of working in the local movie theatre. It wasn't long before the assaults started. It began with seemingly innocent touching, then semi-nudity, then full nudity, and then eventually, full-on rape.

I continued working for him and being sexually abused until I was about seventeen years of age. At this time, I managed to break free. I thought I was really strong for doing this; however, it seemingly wasn't the case as he really didn't care less. He'd surrounded himself with plenty of other young people to play with.

I kept my secret for more than four decades, and I never told a living soul about what'd happened to me. This is EXACTLY the way that perpetrators like it. The first time I spoke with someone about what had happened was some thirty-seven years later, when I was having counselling through the breakdown of my marriage. The counsellor asked me completely out of the blue if anything bad had ever happened to me as a child, such as physical or sexual abuse. Like many people affected by abuse, I lied and emphatically denied such a vulgar suggestion.

This conversation started me thinking over the next few months, and during one of our latter sessions, I reminded my counsellor of the question she had asked me. I then confessed to her that I'd lied and that I in fact had been sexually abused as a child. To my dismay, her response was that she knew ... SHE KNEW! However, she needed me to tell her when I was ready to do so. This small step of opening up to my marriage counsellor was the beginning of my journey of recovery, repair and growth. This little truth started to ripple out and create change across my life.

The focus of my counselling sessions changed. I went on to divulge to my counsellor every detail of my assaults. Until this time, I'd thought that what'd happened to me was horrible, but that it was in the past and I was fine. It had no real effect on my life. How wrong could I have been!

I soon came to realise just how damaged I'd become and how it bubbled up and spilled out into everything I did. I saw how many things that'd happened in my personal and business life were a direct result of the emotional and psychological damage that was inflicted on me as a child. I was in a deep, dark well of pain and shame.

It was also around this time that I heard about the highly

publicised and controversial acquittal of Michael Jackson in his child molestation trial. This travesty, coupled with my new-found understanding of myself, was the tipping point that solidified my resolve to bring my perpetrator to justice – so that I could ensure that he, unlike Jackson, would not be able to use his wealth and privilege to live out his life with impunity.

And so in early 2009, the journey of prosecuting my perpetrator started. It started with that small step of deciding to find my voice and tell my story. A small pebble that was thrown into a very large pond which would ultimately bring my perpetrator to justice. As tough a decision as it was to make, the hardest part was actually following through with my decision. Every day for three months I'd drive to my office telling myself that THIS would be the day – I would make the detour to the police station to report him. And each day as I reached the turn-off to the police station, it was like my car had a mind of its own and it would keep driving straight ahead to my work office.

Each day after this happened, it was like I hated myself even more for being so weak. I hated my perpetrator even more for what he had done to me and the power he still held over me.

Finally in March 2009, I wrestled the car to turn off to the police station. I parked and I went inside. In a very quiet, embarrassed voice, I told the young constable working at the front desk that I wished to report a sexual assault. When he asked me for details, I had to admit that it was me who was affected and that it was nearly some fifty years ago. This was one of the hardest things I'd ever done. And yet, the process had started. It was like a huge burden had been lifted from my shoulders. It became liberating and cathartic to finally tell my story. But would I be believed after such a long period of time?

After weeks of giving statements and investigations by the police, they'd found another nine survivors who'd admitted that they'd been assaulted by the same man. Seven of whom were prepared to provide statements and take the matter to court. That small pebble that I'd thrown into the pond was now rippling outwards and gaining momentum! As it turned out, the size of the case warranted a special police task force being formed, and the police began gathering more evidence and building their case.

I was asked if I'd be prepared to wear a listening device, re-connect with my perpetrator and attempt to gather corroborative evidence – and gain either some admissions or an apology from him.

If I thought that taking the first step into the police station was a tough one, wearing a wire and meeting up with my predator was just off the scale. I agreed, albeit reluctantly and with a great deal of trepidation.

Over the following three-month period I'd meet with my perpetrator weekly, usually over lunch, and each time my heart was racing. I wondered if he could he see my wire and if he suspected me. How could I steer the conversations to gain the evidence I needed? On several occasions he asked about my children, and I told him a little bit about them. He asked to see pictures of them and I ultimately had to show him some pictures that I had on my iPhone, while seeing him grin and leer at them ... knowing the vile thoughts that were going through his mind about MY CHILDREN. It was like stabbing a dagger through my heart.

I managed to gather a lot of corroborative evidence and the police continued to wrap up their case. My perpetrator was finally arrested and charged later in 2009. I can't begin to express the overwhelming joy and pride that I felt when watching his arrest playing out on mainstream news! The man who had accumulated such wealth, privilege and power at the expense and abuse of myself and other children was being taken down. It was my little ripple that began the tsunami that became his downfall.

It'd been a long and difficult journey bringing him to justice, and it was my hope that the courts would deliver a sentence befitting his crimes. However, that wasn't to be. Three years later, the trial began. The wheels of justice really do move at the speed of a glacier. As a result of a decision made by the Crown, my perpetrator was prosecuted in two separate trials. In the first trial, involving myself and another victim, there were twenty-one charges against him. Despite very strong evidence, including the evidence gathered by me during our lunchtime meetings, the jury did not accept this; the Crown did not prove his guilt beyond a reasonable doubt and acquitted him.

This was a gut-wrenching blow, as you can imagine, to both myself and the other victim in this trial. Especially after the torment we'd both endured at his hands as children. It was an emotional rollercoaster to relive these past events throughout the investigation and trial, in addition to me having to endure the trauma of having to "re-connect" with my perpetrator, feign happiness and reminisce over our past.

The second trial involved another five victims and thirty-eight charges, and commenced immediately after my trial. In this trial my perpetrator was found guilty and convicted of all thirty-eight charges. This was a bittersweet pill.

When sentenced, nearly three years after his arrest and after being found guilty of thirty-eight charges – most of which carried sentences ranging from two to ten years and totalling over one hundred years – my perpetrator's time behind bars was to be a maximum of only seven years, with as little as four and a half years.

I was so upset by this gross miscarriage of justice, with his acquittal in my trial and the hopelessly inadequate sentence delivered in his second, that I sent a letter to a radio station and had the matter raised on talkback radio. A few months later, the Office of Public Prosecutors (OPP) successfully ran an appeal against the leniency of my perpetrator's sentence and it was subsequently increased by two years. While it still felt inadequate, it was at least a step in the right direction.

What was highlighted to me throughout this process was that it IS possible to bring about change! My small action of writing to the radio presenter resulted in a ripple that became a successful appeal. I am so very, very grateful to the radio presenter for his passionate support.

As a result of the work that I've done with counsellors in recognising and addressing many of the psychological scars that I've carried throughout my life, I seized back the life power that was stolen from me by my perpetrator – and by throwing that small pebble into the pond that rippled out, I was able to ultimately bring down my perpetrator.

My life has since become enriched and I've finally grown. I've also met and now share my life with the most wonderful woman. The most valuable prize in this process is the ripple effect that my actions have had on others. Other survivors found their voices and had their day in court, and have also been able to begin their journey of recovery.

There have also been others whom I've subsequently shared my story with. This ripple effect is not something that I contemplated at the outset of all of this. But, IT IS REAL, and it will become apparent to every person who stands up and speaks out against CSA.

Let me assure you that EVERY victim of CSA that speaks up WILL CREATE A RIPPLE EFFECT that will add to the wave of change, not only in their own lives, but also for the lives of others and our nation.

And if you are one of the CSA survivors, I encourage you to please come forward. Find your voice and tell your story, and together let's make our country the safest place to raise a child.

RECOGNISING I NEEDED HELP

I didn't tell anyone what had happened
I kept my secret for more than four decades
I waited over thirty years to tell anyone
I was not experiencing growth as a person
I had lost parts of my life, I felt unseen as a father
I looked at my reflection in the mirror....I didn't like what I saw
"What the fuck am I doing with my life?"
The walls I had built in my mind to block out my childhood came crumbling down
A flood of emotions that I had not felt since I was a boy engulfed and consumed me
The uncomfortable feelings inside made it almost unbearable to be in my own skin
I was in a deep, dark well of pain and shame
These feelings began to eat away at the emotional armour that I used to deflect the pain from my childhood trauma
I had an emotional crash.
I soon came to realise just how damaged I'd become
Like many survivors, I have stared into the void of very dark places
I experienced a level of confusion about my sexuality,
what sex is, but also about attraction and arousal
It is difficult for people who have not experienced sexual abuse to comprehend
the magnitude of the devastating effect that it can have on a person
And no matter how much I would talk, I still felt like there was unfinished business.
I still did not know how to tell my partner about the abuse.
Over time, memories came back
I remember saying that it was enough

It's important to recognise how we fought what the abuse
What it told us, taught us and conditioned us to be
I remind myself that I managed to break free
What is important is that I have survived and can tell my story
Hope returned once I sought help

FOLLOW THE YELLOW BRICK ROAD

BRAYDEN CRANE (HE/HIM)

My name is Brayden, my pronouns are he/him and I am a survivor of child sexual abuse. This is my story of who I came to be and how, following sixteen years on from that awful and traumatic night in my bedroom as an eleven year old boy.

It is September 2019 and I am laying on the couch typing up my story as my partner of almost ten years lays on the second couch, playing a video game. Video games have been a big part of both of our lives growing up. We met when I was seventeen and I was homeless interstate. We have now lived on the east coast together for eight years. I was homeless as a result of my dad kicking me out of home. I'm still not 100 percent sure of the reason why he kicked me out, but I'm fairly confident it was because I was gay. I had come out to my family and friends barely six months before, and although I could tell that Dad was trying really hard to accept who I was, it was obvious to me that he was also fighting with it internally.

I was homeless, studying Year 12 full time and working permanent part time while sleeping on the floor of a family friends' house. Around the same time, I managed to lose my

BRAYDEN CRANE (HE/HIM)

wallet on a bus on my way home from work, which (luckily for me) led me to meeting the love of my life, and resulted in a chain of fortunate events that have led me to where I now find myself.

I truly believe that all humans exist to help and support each other, and as much as I love helping others in absolutely any way that I can, it can be incredibly taxing – physically, mentally and emotionally. I have been trying to take less responsibility for everybody else's happiness and focus more on me, but I find it really hard. I feel like, "If I don't help them, who will?" I get that I have to set boundaries and that I "can't save everyone", but helping is at the core of who I am. It may be very closely tied to my experience as a survivor of child sexual abuse, and I'm working on doing more for me, but here I am yet again, hoping to help others through their journey of healing by sharing my own story.

In all honesty, sharing my story is helping me with my own healing and giving me the strength to continue to live with what happened, and to channel that strength toward being a better me for my friends, my family, my partner and well ... me.

When I was eleven – or around then, it's hard to pinpoint when exactly – I was sexually abused in my bedroom. Everybody in the house was asleep – well, everybody apart from "him". He was a friend of my Dad's, and I think Mum's also, but she wasn't living with us at that point in time. He didn't have a consistent presence in our lives, but he was consistent enough that we knew who he was when he would randomly rock up on our doorstep with his camera around his neck. He was always great with my older sisters and me, and from memory he had his own children, but for some reason he did not have custody of them.

One night he once again appeared at our doorstep, and as always, we were excited to see him, as he was always hilarious and a heap of fun. Thinking about him now makes me feel anxious, incredibly tight in my chest and sick in my stomach. The twins and I had gone to bed after an hour or so of him arriving; we all had our own bedrooms while Dad slept in the lounge room. Dad sacrificed a lot for us kids and he did everything for us, before himself. I wasn't aware that Dad's friend would be staying over for the night.

Seeing as Dad took up the lounge room and that it wouldn't be appropriate to place him in the room of young girls, the only other option was my room. I had no idea that he had even been placed on a spare mattress on my bedroom floor until he woke me up. I was fast asleep in my car bed; they were super cool even if I never was interested in cars.

My sleep had been interrupted by noise coming from the bedroom floor. I looked over the edge of my bed and saw him crying. I was always a very caring and thoughtful kid, and growing up, the sight of somebody crying upset me immensely. I always wanted people to be happy and I hated seeing people sad or upset. I asked him if he was okay, and he replied that he wasn't and that he missed his kids. He continued to say something along the lines of, "What I wouldn't give to hug my kids again," and how it would make him feel better if somebody gave him a hug. Surely giving him a hug would be fine; he'd stop crying, and I could go back to sleep. I got out of bed to hug and console him. He then pulled me under the covers and against his bare skin. He said it was okay. All he was wearing were his underpants.

What I thought was an innocent hug led to him kissing me, and him then telling me to kiss his penis because it would make him feel better, to him then pushing it to my mouth. Everything becomes a little hazy when I try to recall what happened, but one thing I do remember is saying that it was enough and getting back into my own bed. This was followed by endless statements from him, such as, "Don't tell anybody or you'll get in a lot of trouble." I was more than happy to agree. I thought I had done something really wrong.

BRAYDEN CRANE (HE/HIM)

When I woke the next morning, he was gone. Dad didn't even see him leave. I was relieved as I didn't have to face him, and I didn't until a year or so later.

I was at a friend's house and he was walking past as I walked out. He started yelling out that he loved me and that he wanted to hug me. My friend and his mum were confused about what was going on. I didn't want them to find out what happened. I ran back into their house, out the back door, jumped the fence into the backyard of another house, jumped another, and then another until I managed to get back to where we were living at the time. I didn't want him to know where we had moved to. That was the last time that I saw or heard from him, until four years later when I told my Mum and Dad what had happened that night.

I don't really recall how I felt following that night, other than hoping that nobody would find out, because I would surely be in a lot of trouble. One night, I eventually decided to tell my Dad what had happened, when I was feeling really low about being rejected by a girl at school I thought I liked. I was still trying to convince myself that I was straight at that point. My Dad and his then girlfriend (now wife) reacted with anger towards him and made statements such as, "I will hunt him down and kill him." The following day I went to my Mum's house and I also shared my experiences with her, and she responded similarly.

I'm not sure if anybody asked me if I wanted to report the abuse to the police, but as far as I'm aware, it was never reported. At the time I think that I was happy to get it out and move on, but some part of me wishes that we did report it, and that he got what he deserved. I also kind of wanted my parents to put their words into action; to hunt him down and to make him pay, and then I also wanted people to forget about it and not talk about it again. And nobody did.

Around the time that it happened, I made friends with a kid at school who introduced me to a video game called *Final*

Fantasy VIII (8). I was absolutely in awe of the visuals, and I thought that it was incredibly realistic. The characters, the story and the music drew me into a world that allowed me to escape my reality. It offered a story that made me feel like I was part of the world that was on my screen, regardless of how pixelated it was. I had the same experience with *The Wizard of Oz*, which was introduced to me after another traumatic experience in my life when I was about five years old.

The ability to escape my world and join Dorothy and the gang on their journey to become wiser, more caring, more courageous and more daring was something that I constantly sought. I was drawn to Dorothy's ability to step up for those who needed her help and for standing up for what she believed in. I was inspired by her strength and resilience. *The Wizard of Oz* and *Final Fantasy VIII* in particular brought me joy, while also providing some sense of escape and reassurance that things really do get better.

Each and every person deals with trauma in their own way, and I am still processing my own, but I am glad that I have finally started to work through it. In 2018, I saw an Instagram post of somebody participating in the Polished Man campaign, and within that post they shared that they were a survivor of child sexual abuse. It immediately triggered my own experience, and paired with my constant need to help others, it motivated me to take part and fundraise for a campaign to support children who have experienced violence and/or abuse.

I then shared with my partner, of eight and a half years at the time, my experience as an eleven year old boy. I was nervous that he would distance himself from me, thinking that I was dirty and the last person he would want to be with. He did distance himself for a short while, but upon reflection, that had more to do with him providing me with the space I needed to process finally addressing my experience as a child. He was incredibly supportive and ensured that each time I shared or spoke about it, I was in control of what I wanted to share, when, and how much.

I would like for young people who are reading this and have been through something similar to know that I believe in you. Believe that you are strong. Believe that you can overcome this. Believe that you are loved and have so much to offer this world. This experience only adds to who you are, and to your ability to live with your experience shows your immense strength. Find someone or something that gives you this constant reminder, because there will be days where you don't believe a word of this – but please know that you have the strength to get through anything.

I wish my parents told us about saying "no" to unwanted attention and to know how to recognise inappropriate behaviour. While growing up, we certainly had conversations about stranger danger and not taking things from strangers and so on, but this person was known to our family. I wish I knew more about how to protect myself at the time. Please know that it is okay to say "no", know that your body belongs to you, and know that you don't ever have to do anything you don't want to. Their actions are not your fault; whatever happened is not your fault. There is love and support around you.

My journey along the yellow brick road has been traumatic for sure, but it has also been exciting – full of love, success and many, many laughs. Overcoming this obstacle only adds to my strength as a person, and there will be many more positives along the journey that will help me maintain hope that things get better. Things are already better since I have opened up about my story, and I know that I can grow even stronger. I can and will be the best me, and this experience does not define me. Following the yellow brick road has brought me this far and it only gets better from here.

My name is Brayden and I am a survivor of child sexual abuse.

I HELD SOME UNHELPFUL BELIEFS

I held some unhelpful beliefs. I was taught these things
This is how sexual abuse works, how it teaches you to feel
Or how you see yourself or worrying about how I am being judged
I was never good enough
I blamed myself for my abuse
Being raped was punishment for being weak
I felt that I would be viewed as weak if I spoke
Speaking out was a sign of being even weaker
These things don't happen to men. If they do, we tell no-one
I felt that being a man, I wasn't ever supposed to tell anyone about what had happened
I thought I had done something really wrong, I thought that it was partly my fault
I couldn't tell. I didn't even try to make sense of what was happening to me
I wholeheartedly believed that I was not able to say anything about the abuse
I was helpless, powerless, submissive and a confused mess for much of my childhood
I was scared of being around other kids at school, I was ashamed of what happened
Surrounded every day by boys who reminded me of those dark years, it pushed me over the edge
I wasn't complicit in the abuse. I resisted the abuse by trying to fight back
As a child, I had never felt 'seen' by those who mattered most to me
I had no self-belief, I thought that suicide was easier than telling even one person
Boys who are victims of childhood sexual abuse are [often] faced with gender identity problems

Men who have been sexually abused may experience sexual confusion about their sexual preferences

Being a victim goes against our society's norms of what it is to be a man

I knew that I would never find peace if I didn't overcome my experiences

I had to figure out how to manage my suffering and my past

I had to reprogram my mind, I didn't know why – but I knew I had to start

Overcoming this obstacle adds to my strength as a person

I knew that it would be worth it

The past can haunt you, but cannot hurt you

Everything you do to move forward takes the power away from your perpetrator

Your experience doesn't have to define you, this was not your fault

The only person who should be blamed is the perpetrator

It is possible to bring about change

Every victim of childhood sexual abuse that speaks up will create a ripple effect that will add to the wave of change

Your opinion of yourself is all that matters, and your past does not define you

So don't ever stop fighting and don't ever lose hope

You are always worthy and strong, and you always will be

When you survive, you become like a tree in a storm....the deeper your roots grow, the stronger you become

I'm still standing, I'm still strong and I always will be

I control my life, and I control my happiness

I can decide who I want to be and I will

There will always be sunshine coming someday soon

The little boy within, he was both traumatised and filled with shame

But the power of love would always triumph over the love of power

Sometimes we don't ever heal our wounds entirely, scars or pain remain

But instead of hating my body, I can say I love and accept myself just the way I am

It might feel like you're lost, or missing

But I've learnt that it's okay to lose ourselves before we find ourselves

There is no escaping you, so you might as well be your own best friend

Find a sense of yourself that you know is your own and be true to that part of yourself and nurture it

Don't blame yourself – the greatest healing powers are love and forgiveness

I am being a better me for my friends, my family, my partner....me

I am no longer afraid of what of what had happened, nor am I ashamed

If you look, you will find that there truly is gold everywhere

LINE IN THE SAND

MAL

As I write today, I am sitting in my little 60 square metre home that we have spent the last twelve months putting together on our 5500 square metre property. With all of our hard work, I just relocated our water tank, so that we have beautiful clean rain water pouring into our tank. At this rate it will nearly be full by this afternoon, fingers crossed. I am snuggled comfortably on our lounge with my dog Lille on my lap.

Lille saved my life back in August 2017 when I had a seizure, which was only four weeks before my trial. You see, I had come home late from my monthly men's group and I went upstairs to check in on my partner and to give her a kiss. I then went downstairs, as I was struggling with sleep apnea at the time and I was feeling hyper-vigilant. Next thing, I woke up in hospital some eighteen hours later. If Lille hadn't responded to my seizure and ran to wake my partner, I wouldn't be here today telling you my Restoring Hope journey.

I grew up in a family experiencing domestic violence and this broke my childhood. This was when the abuse started; however, because of my family's situation, I was stuck in a protective survival mode. I couldn't escape and even though I did try to tell others, I wasn't believed. So I just internalised everything that was happening in my life. I went to live in foster care, where I felt alone. I then moved into institutions and then I eventually lived on the streets.

This was all by the time I was fifteen years old. I had experienced thirteen years of abuse, including five years of unwarranted sexual abuse. I was an orphan by eight years of age. I did not think that I would make it to twenty years old, and never did I imagine making it to thirty, forty or in my wildest thoughts back then, that I would be in the position I am sitting now, reflecting back and to be able to say, "Hang in there, you will do amazing things." And for me to know that I have overcome and done these things.

Growing up for me was truly about survival. I avoided focusing on what had happened in my life during this time for over thirty years. Then one day, I was approached and I made a decision that ultimately changed my life. Through many years of counselling, and through meeting some amazing people whom I felt that I could trust at once, I have slowly been able to share a little about my experience of sexual abuse.

I have always been a self-educated and good man. I have never been in trouble with the law. I have always been into extreme challenges, be it through work or play. I am an upstanding citizen and a hard worker. However, I never felt normal and I felt left behind in life.

If I were to start thanking everyone who has helped me along the way, I would have a very long list of people to thank. While going through my journey, I have been fortunate to be selective with whom I would speak to and what I would speak about, and I would have very controlled analytical conversations with those around me. I wasn't aware of this at the time, but it has served me well throughout my entire life. I have survived – and sadly, many people don't.

Because of this, I pay homage to those who, for whatever reason, did not, could not or cannot speak today about what has happened to them. Sadly, I thought I was the only one who had been through what I had, and I wasn't.

I feel that how others respond to what has happened depends a lot on yourself and how safe you feel inside and with those in your life. For me, when I went through the judiciary system, I chose to keep my partner aware and up to date with what was happening; however, I preferred for her to remain at home. I wanted her to feel full of happiness, love and support when I arrived home. I wanted to leave the justice matters at the door, so I studied and used my counsellor to help me to retrain my thinking about how to best handle the situation. With everything you hear and learn, you cannot change if you don't take action on it. Change has to come from the inside and then filter outwards. I wanted change, so I made change happen for me.

Advice that I would give others experiencing something similar to me is to make sure that you educate yourself as much as possible. Do not be defined by those who betray you, because when you survive, you become like a tree in a storm – and the harder that things seem, the deeper your roots become. And there will always be sunshine coming someday soon.

I have been sharing about my childhood and raising awareness that we can speak up and say that sexual abuse is not okay; in fact, that any abuse is not okay. If I were to know that someone had been in a similar position to me, I would speak up and do what I can to give them a voice.

I now live in the bush and have found that going back to nature has helped me in so many ways. I had to get away from the city because where I lived, I was constantly reminded of events that had happened, just by driving along my daily commute. This wasn't helping me and it definitely wasn't healthy for me.

These days, I feel okay, and while I still have my bad days, there are not many. I find purpose in watching and learning about science, nature, evolution, and life – and this is what it is all about now for me. I now am able to wake up in the morning and I walk onto our front verandah to see birds, pretty-faced wallabies and green trees, and I feel a fresh south-easterly breeze from the coast.

A good book of reference is called *Surviving the Legal System* by Caroline Taylor[1]. I would also like to mention a thank you to some very important people who walked with me through my journey and are now some of my dearest friends: Danny Keen and Michel Usher from Channel 9's *60 Minutes*, Craig Hughes Cashmore from "SAMSN", and Gary Foster from "Living Well" and his team of truly amazing people. I have also many more to thank.

Through my journey I have had the pleasure to give feedback about my experiences, and I feel that this tool alone helps a lot.

Everyone has their own ways of dealing with trauma. Some people externalise and some people internalise their experiences, but usually it is a blend of both. The outcome is that everybody is individual, so the best way to start is to treat one another as human.

At least for today, I sit and write to you knowing that help is easier to access than it was during my childhood. This is why I want to share my journey with others.

LINE IN THE SAND

WALKING WITH YOU

CLINTON ALLMAN

I am a loving father, a husband, a son, a brother, an uncle, and a child sexual abuse survivor. I am forty-seven years old at the time of writing this brief overview of my life's moments, as seen through my eyes, as a survivor. I have lived through over thirty-five years of daily torment due to the sexual abuse I endured as a child by my perpetrator. It is difficult to know where to begin and where to end. What is important is that I have survived and can tell my story. I hope that my story enables other survivors to start or continue to heal, and know that we all walk together even if on different paths

Despite my abhorrent childhood, I ask myself many questions on a daily basis. How did I make it to today? How did I keep taking steps forward? Where did my resilience come from? What has kept me going? Why is it that I now see a brighter future?

My story is not one of institutional child sexual abuse, but one of sexual abuse by a family "friend". A trusted man who infiltrated my family and my world. Grooming that was so effective and contrived, no one could see what was happening right before their eyes. He became part of my family, my extended family and their friends' lives. The trust afforded to him was so great that he was able to regularly sleep in another bed in my bedroom, take me out on a whim, away from the eyes of my parents at home, and even on overnight trips and holidays that would last up to a week.

I wholeheartedly believed that I was not able to say anything about the abuse. He was seen by my family and their friends as a saint. To me, he was part of "an inner circle of trust" that I could not break for fear of some sort of severe punishment, or simply not being believed. I was helpless, powerless, submissive and a confused mess for much of my childhood. He held all the power. In my mind, I was somehow an outsider within my own family.

It was in the early 1980s when the sexual abuse began. I was a nine year old powerless, impressionable and quiet young boy. My family and I went on a holiday together with other families and friends of my perpetrator. A family holiday should be a normal activity for families to do. The beach, surf, barbeques, family and friends – but throughout those years, my perpetrator was a constant and central presence, no matter where we were.

Relentless silent embarrassment and humiliation sat with me, weighing me down and causing me to isolate myself from others. I was branded with pet names by my perpetrator, which led me to feel that I was the exclusive property of a child abuser. I hid the shame from my family. I was scared and ashamed of being around other kids at school. I had no one whom I could call a friend. I held a tremendous sense of fear and confusion around everyone who saw me with him. I had no idea who I could turn to or tell. These facts alone help address that number one question that survivors are always asked: "Why didn't you tell someone?"

As I grew older, the fear of being blamed, shamed, not believed, called names, and having everyone know what had happened, and continued to happen, filled me with dread.

The impact on my life has been overwhelmingly devastating, placing enormous strain on my own wellbeing, and all too often on those around me as well. The joy and innocence of my childhood, and my teen years, were taken away. I, like many survivors, have stared into the void of very dark places on many occasions, made vulnerable in other situations, and I had been driven to behaviours that I would not ordinarily have undertaken.

Feeling alone and determined not to accept help from anyone, I shut out my family. I grew angrier and more frustrated each and every day, wondering why those around me could not see the obvious, even as the years ticked by. All the while, the sexual abuse was becoming a normalised part of my life, no longer something I expected, but something I had to accept as part of my everyday existence.

Holding the weight of the abuse within me, not on my shoulders but in my mind and my mental state for over thirty-five years has been overpowering. As I woke up each and every day, the abuse took up a part of my brain capacity, putting me behind others. It's something that no survivor should have to endure. To this day, I do not know how I, initially as a nine year old, coped with the puzzling world around me. I don't think I will ever know exactly how I muddled through life, but here I am!

By 2017, I was struggling so much that I was close to breaking down again. Piece by piece, the wall I had built in my mind to block out my childhood, came crumbling down. I was at the point where something had to be done, not just for myself, but also for my family and those around me. For decades, since the abuse first occurred, I thought I was alone and I had to do everything myself; I did not accept help from others even when it was offered. In fact, I made it my mission. Just one consequence of dealing with the abuse as a child. It stands to reason that I did not open up about it.

Three years ago, I found something deep inside of me

that pushed the shame, the embarrassment, and the blame aside. I took action and reached out for support. I sought professional help, rather than continuing to deal with it alone. It was only then that I finally knew I would be believed and maybe, just maybe, even supported.

There have been a number of events that have changed my life. One of the most significant was when I listened to a radio clip posted on social media. It was by an ambassador of a child abuse organisation, talking about his perpetrator, his life, and how he had overcome his own experiences and mental demons. He happened to work in a similar industry to my own. With my wife pleading with me to reach out, I typed a message, asking him to connect and hopefully listen to my story. After thirty minutes or more of my finger hovering over the "send" and the "delete" button, I shut my eyes and finally sent it.

Boom – a giant step that I had not been able to do for thirty-five years. I actually asked someone for help! My emotions were high; I was feeling overwhelmed, regretful, nervous, relieved, exhilarated and worried all at once.

To my surprise, the following morning, he replied. I was tense as I opened the message. "He will not want to help or support me; he will give me a standard email wishing me all the best. He will just ... hold on, are my eyes deceiving me? He wants to catch up the next time he is in my city, which just in a few short weeks time!" To my amazement, he had also made some initial enquiries for me.

In less than twelve hours I had begun to turn around a thirty-five year ordeal. I was gobsmacked. "Someone wants to help me?" I couldn't believe it. As I found out, there are actually those who want to help! The healing had finally begun!

My first meeting with him gave me hope. A lot of hope. The kind of unwavering hope that "the Resistance" has when battling the Empire. I told him how alone I felt carrying the burden, and about the guilt and shame that has sat with me for so long. He told me that I had taken the first step of many – one that will now find me with a lot of support, and supporters around me. I felt a level of comfort that I had never felt before. This was a defining moment for me. Not only was I believed, but I was also supported and backed by a fellow survivor who had already helped so many others. Our chat didn't quite last an hour, but it was all it took to provide me with my first shred of confidence. I was blown away, as a lightning bolt shot through me that I should have reached out for support long ago

The following week, he promptly followed up on our discussion, and asked me one of the toughest questions I have ever been asked ... and just like that, I was talking to the police interstate, arranging a time to make a statement. He also put me onto a specialist men's counselling service, who referred me to another service, which took me in quickly knowing that I was about to make a statement. A whirlwind hit me that in many ways I was unprepared for, but I also knew that I could not take another step backwards. As quickly as this occurred, I always maintain that it happened thirty-five years too slowly!

Making my statement was an emotional rollercoaster in itself. I very quickly had my first counselling session, followed by a flight interstate to make my statement. Over the prior weeks I had recalled many events, some in extreme minute detail through a combination of photos, events that occurred, or through vivid memories and flashbacks. I was not prepared to go into the detail that I did. I was not expecting to be at the police station all day, then visiting the following day to finish and sign the statement. I was absolutely mentally and emotionally spent, and yet I felt elated that I pushed through it. It was done.

If you go down this path, be prepared to relive your story, your chronology of events, and the minute details. It is not an easy experience. If you do, be prepared that you may also feel like you have done the right thing by you, possibly other victims and the community ... but especially YOU.

Over the years, I had a few false starts at wanting to put myself through counselling, but it always fell over at the last hurdle. Maybe I wasn't ready, maybe I was scared, maybe I was not brave enough, or maybe I was just unsure how I would react, and that I might question whether it would all really help. Taking this step has in fact helped me enormously, and it is one of the reasons I have been able to forge a road of healing and recovery. Having someone to listen to, someone to speak with in confidence and who understands, and someone to provide guidance has made all of the difference.

Counselling helped me before and after making my statement. Monthly "drop-in" groups were organised, where I could join other survivors from all walks of life. I was able to sit and listen, contribute if I wanted to and drop in when I felt like it, with no expectation to describe or discuss any detail of my own abuse. Although groups like this are not for everyone, just turning up to this group helped me when I needed it the most. The group has also allowed me to connect with like-minded survivors, allowing me to help and support them, while also assisting with my own healing process.

The positive "knock-on" effects of making the statement has been massive and out-weighed the necessity of reliving my traumatic childhood. Four other victims made their own statements, which lead to over forty charges. A little over a year later, our perpetrator was arrested. This led to guilty pleas and sentencing. The sentence handed down was for sixteen years with twelve years non-parole, l. At the end of the day, I took the step, which allowed four others to do the same. The perpetrator is now in jail.

While this outcome has allowed a door to be partially

closed, it will never be closed completely. I have accepted that. I will not lie, the past three years since making my statement have seen some of the most difficult days of my life, and had it not been for counselling and support, I certainly would have had some very different outcomes. That said, knowing that I did eventually do "the right thing" for myself, the other victims and the community provides me with the knowledge that a level of safety has been restored in the community – the other survivors and I have now been able to begin our healing process.

Meeting the other survivors at court helped me enormously on my road to recovery. Initially, I was unsure of their reaction as I was the one to drag out the spectre of days gone by, thrusting it into the front of the mind of other survivors. I was pleasantly surprised and humbled to be told that I had changed their lives. That I was a "hero" for taking the step, enabling them to join in and tell their story to investigating officers. I simply see that I was someone who needed to speak out to help myself, along with the other survivors who endured child sexual abuse.

While not for everyone, I lifted my media suppression order to ensure that others heard another survivor's voice, with the hope that this would help others heal, speak out, seek support or even bring their perpetrator to account. I thought that speaking in front of a news camera would be way out of my comfort zone, but it was made much easier knowing that the outcome would be to help others, raise awareness, and provide another voice. I want all survivors to know that they will be believed and supported.

As I started my road to healing, I have looked to help other survivors in any way possible. I believe this also helps me to recover and heal. It is as simple as meeting other survivors over a coffee and just talking about whatever comes up at the time. I feel comfort in knowing that there is a shared understanding and support for each other.

What I advocate is for survivors to know that there is now greater community awareness, access to a number of safe organisations, and more confidence in the investigative and legal processes, even though there is still a fair way to go. I encourage you not to let the abuse continue to be a normalised part of your life (as I  allowed for so long), or a constant presence in your life. No child should be subjected to any form of abuse, whether that is sexual, physical, emotional or otherwise. Please speak out and seek support.

Reaching out to someone changed my life, as it started the process of healing for me. Sometimes it came with two steps forward and one step backwards, and sometimes with ten steps backwards. It has now led me to a path where I can advocate for survivors, and let survivors know that there is support and many ways to walk the path of hope and healing.

I am managing in life now with the support of my family. Having attended three years of counselling. I am now better equipped to manage my triggers and the difficulties of living through life after being sexually abused as a child.

To quote my Victim impact statement, "Today is another day. A day where I am hopeful that as I look back in the months and years ahead, I see today as a step forward." I hope that if you are a survivor or someone currently experiencing sexual abuse, or abuse of any kind, my story will help you find support and take the first step forward... I walk with you.

HEALING BEGAN

I sought professional help without knowing exactly what I was asking for
It started with that small step of deciding to find my voice and tell my story
....to start, or continue to heal
I took action on that decision
A conversation with my friend was the turning point
We weren't real close as friends, but they made me feel very comfortable, allowing me to drop my barriers
That phone call saved my life
She needed me to tell her when I was ready to
She believed me. She said I was brave
Being brave and speaking out has been the hardest part
Change began with me telling my story
Once I started, it all just flowed out
It became liberating and cathartic to finally tell my story
It wasn't quite as easy as I thought it would be.
A friend reached out and told me that he too was a victim
Seeing me speak out gave him hope and strength for his own recovery
Though our stories were different, our wounds were near identical.
Hitting rock bottom became a good foundation to build and grow from
The real healing started the moment that I was informed that I wasn't responsible
It gave me recognition that sexual abuse shouldn't happen
I was not the failure that I thought I was
I spent several years climbing the steep path out of the deep, bleak valley of desolation
I was able to label my emotions when times became difficult

I came to understand that there was no danger of abuse any more
I have learned not to blame myself
I have moved from locking it away to having quite regular thoughts about it
I now feel sufficiently recovered that I can, and want to, assist others in their recovery and healing
I have a role to play in society
I have recovered to a point where I can work and live as effectively as before
It does get easier to live with
My healing from childhood sexual abuse is not finished
And I would not have made it alone, the journey of recovery is lifelong
But I am continuing to give it a go and I am taking steps in my recovery and healing
And these small steps bring me closer to the bright future I'd hoped for.

THE DANCER

ANDREW MOURNEHIS

*J*oseph Campbell once said we all share ONE GREAT STORY! A universal story called *The Hero's Journey*[1].

My story had been told a thousand times, and kept me bound to the minutiae of a tortured tale!

By turning my story into a myth, it has provided distance, relief and a broader perspective of my history – and in a strangely healing way, released me from the shackles of my trauma, bringing with it greater freedom and deeper meaning.

This myth is a universal tale touching on themes such as loss of innocence, sexual abuse, bullying, loneliness, disease, addiction and spiritual awakening.

By transmuting the poisons of the past, I discovered the medicine of dance, spirituality, yoga, chanting, meditation, transpersonal therapy and other alternative holistic approaches that have been incredibly healing.

The greatest healing powers, however, have been love and forgiveness, and to that I truly surrender.

I believe the power of transposing our story into a myth

is that we get the opportunity to write the end of it, so we may live more powerfully into our future. A future not yet in full manifestation, but co-created with the universe – bringing with it unexpected gifts, that we may eventually share with others.

This myth is a gift of love and I hope it offers a message to you.

As Joseph Campbell once said, our myths are "truer than truth".

"The Dancer" is you and me ... yours and mine ... and will live for all of time ...

THE DANCER

A Tiny Dancer entered the world with music in his soul. His language was melody and his song was divine.

Cherished and precious, His mama prayed every day to the angels for his safety and loved him so dearly that his namesake was offered to the Saint of Miracles.

However, within the safe world of melodies lived a demon whose ways were sinister. He circled the vulnerable boy, penetrating his sacred earth, damaging his fertile soil, while echoes of laughter wafted in the stale air. His creative ground now contaminated and cursed became quicksand that kept pulling him under. Evil eyes and conniving kisses wounded the delicate soul, and his view of love became skewed and confused.

The music inside him died ... and so did the dance. He was both traumatised and filled with shame.

As he grew up he would walk heavily, dragging his chubby flat feet. Clumsy and lost in the dark, he tripped and stumbled downstairs into a black hole, where snakes slithered and lecherous old trolls salivated over blood dripping from his open wounds. The portal of darkness was open and the door to death was ready and waiting, with the dark forces pushing him to the edge of shame.

Pills, potions, promiscuity and poisons plagued the poor performer onto a stage with no lights. The wings provided no safety. The orchestra played haunting sounds like violins with broken strings, and there seemed to be no "exit stage left" to be seen!

He knew the light of love would lead him home but he could not find the stage door. He looked for it in the elders but they were not wise. He looked for it in fantasies and fetishes but they created more illusions. He cried for his mama but her love only appeared close to death. Death's door had opened and he was being ushered through.

He saw a light as he prepared to transition to the other side; he was in awe of the light of love, which was beautiful, luminous and filled with the sweetest sounds. Here, he knew, he could dance for all eternity, with angels and saints and those who'd passed the threshold before him.

Then in the blink of an eye, in one fleeting moment, the light dissolved and he was back in his weak, pain-ridden body. Mama wept at his feet. The spotlight had turned on and he could finally see himself on the stage: battered, abandoned, alone and afraid. His eyes could not unsee what they had seen, and he clung to the glimpse of pure love from the other side like a lifeline! It reassured him and dissolved the fear of death for the remaining years of his life.

As he grew older and stronger and was able to walk again, men from the audience came to ask him to dance, offering their hand, but they knew not how to dance the "Dance of Love". Each man betrayed him, abandoned him and violated him. The tones of demons past stuck to his soul and wouldn't release him from their grasp.

One thing was clear: each man who came to dance reflected something back to him that he himself was too ashamed to bare. The cloaks he wrapped around himself to conceal the truth on stage also concealed the love that was deep inside his soul.

The Tiny Dancer was small and vulnerable – and the demons and trolls were large, ominous and filled with a lust that drained his poor young soul of life force.

Only the "Dance of Love" would set him free, for it was in his blood and would never leave him. It gave him life! Only the "Dance of Love" would fill his cup and provide salvation and Freedom.

Through a twist of fate, a book of miracles fell at his feet, and a healing path was revealed to him. A miraculous course filled with lessons of love and forgiveness.

The first lesson he learned from the book was that "miracles would occur when he would shift his perception from fear to love". The second lesson was that "forgiveness was the key to freedom".

And so each day he prayed; each day he transformed fear. Each day he took another step along the path of forgiveness, and each courageous step he took released another veil from his heavy layered cloak and his soul felt lighter. His steps were less laboured and he started to hear a calling – faint at first, but then the voices got louder. The deities began calling him, singing their sweet odes, calling him to dance with them …

The light began to get stronger on the stage. The demons could not compete with the light of love, and with the power of so many deities he was reminded that the power of love would always triumph over the love of power.

The more he danced with the loving deities, the more his veils fell to the earth, making the sand solid under his feet once more. He danced the dance of pure love and saw the love inside him.

… And then one day, love came. When he least expected it.

THE DANCER

His beloved asked him to dance. He placed a ring on his finger, made heartfelt vows and they danced the "Dance of Love", as Shiva and Shakti had.

... They danced and they danced and they danced ... and they danced ... together for all eternity ... They danced ...

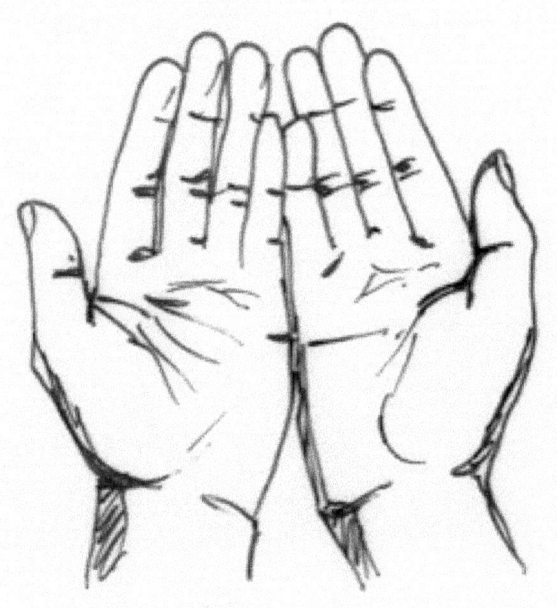

INSIGHTS

JOHN SPENDER

I was so excited to have my aunty and uncle come and visit us at our home on the Central Coast, an hour north of Sydney. They had flown across from their home base in Perth and were staying in the area. I have so many fond memories of growing up and having my uncle in my life. We would often wrestle, and on the last night of their trip, I was wrestling with my uncle while my mum and aunty were chatting in the adjacent dining room a few feet away, having a couple of drinks but nothing too heavy.

What began as a harmless wrestle quickly transformed into a complete violation of my body as my uncle held me down, pulled my grey PJ pants around my knees, and shoved an ice cube up my bum. Being around 14, I still wasn't strong enough to resist my uncle, who is 6'1 with a solid build. My mother and aunt were watching and laughing while I tried to cover my penis so they wouldn't see it. I tried in vain to stop my uncle from ice cubing my butt. It was a shocking feeling when he put the ice in my anus. I immediately wanted to take it out, but it had melted.

My aunty looked shocked and could see that I wasn't okay with what just happened. My mum was still laughing, seemly oblivious to my discomfort and what had occurred. I was embarrassed and confused by the situation as feelings of humiliation washed over my body. I didn't have the emotional intelligence to express how I truly felt about the sexual abuse. On reflection, I can see now that keeping it to myself only made matters worse. Not long after the incident, I started getting high and self-medicating on cannabis weekly. I would wag school and get drunk with my friends while still holding down a part-time job. I became a lot quieter and more withdrawn. This became my pattern for many years. The drugs became harder and stronger and I surprisedly had periods of financial success. Even going on epic travel trips couldn't quite mask the empty feeling that I often felt.

"Destroy the idea that repressing emotions is a sign of strength."
~ Unknown

The whole experience was weird and a little creepy and left me feeling confused about my sexuality. Lucky for me, this was an isolated incident, and my relationship with my uncle had always been good. Unfortunately, many sexual assault victims aren't so fortunate as they live with their perpetrators; their lives become a living hell. I also believe that we shouldn't minimize sexual misconduct and the negative lasting impression of the victim. Sexual abuse is sexual abuse, although there are different degrees of intensity. Even though I would say my case is on the milder side, it affected me more than I could possibly imagine. Having suppressed what had happened deep into my subconscious mind, it wasn't until I attended a personal development event in 2010 that the memories came flooding back.

While listening to the main speaker, I was triggered to share his sexual abuse story with such intensity and sadness. This occurred on the first day and I felt like leaving the four-day seminar. My uncomfortable feelings inside made it almost unbearable to be in my own skin. However, there was something in the tone and the eye contact from the speaker that made me stay. I'm glad I did. Otherwise, I would have missed out on joining the speaker's 12-month coach the coach training. It was a decent investment of 38k. I remember shaking while signing the contract.

The timing was right as a month earlier. I had an epiphany celebrating Australia Day at the Bondi Hotel. We had been doing lines of cocaine in the bathroom. I remember it like it was yesterday. I was watching my mate wipe the top of the toilet seat, sprinkling the powder and raking it into four lines as I rolled a fifty-dollar note ready to snort the coke. This process is done reasonably quickly as not to attract too much attention. As I was cleaning my nose with water, I looked at my reflection in the mirror that stretched the length of the rectangular bathroom and I didn't like what I saw. I felt like I couldn't get enough of what I despised. There and then, I committed to myself that I would do whatever it took to become a better man. Finally, I took action on that decision. I had been self-medicating on drugs and alcohol in different forms and levels since I was 12. I knew that I needed to make significant changes to how I was showing up in the world. I was tired of disappointing myself.

Armed with commitment and determination, the 12-month coaching program became a genuine turning point for me. I began to peel the layers of guilt, fear and shame from my physic at a much deeper level than I had ever done before I dabbled in personal development programs. The first challenge I overcame was showing up to the group calls. I experienced strong feelings of fear and anxiety. I wanted to stay small and miss the calls altogether, but I remained sturdy and showed up no matter what. I was quiet in the beginning as I became use to the energy of the group and the other coaches. The consistency I was stepping out of my comfort zone led to many transformations and personal growth. Once you stretch a rubber band, it never returns to its original size, and that was definitely the case for me.

"No matter how far you go in the wrong direction, there is always a chance to turn your life around." ~ Unknown

I completed the coach the coach program with two NLP certifications, over 270 hours of training, three months of pro bono work at Mission Australia working with people in crisis situations, sold my landscape gardening business that I had for 11 years and began my own flourishing coaching practice. I also spoke on stage at three events in Brisbane, Perth, the Gold Coast and so much more goodness came into my life when I said yes to that coaching program. Even though I had many epic breakthroughs, I learned that I'm still evolving with emotional triggers and wounds. I'm okay with not being okay or not knowing the answer to something, or having everything figured out. Show me someone that does and I'll run the other way! And don't get me wrong, it still can be emotional owing the trauma and not letting it own you through unconscious behavioural patterns.

I remember when Michelle first asked me to contribute to this book and talk about my sexual abuse incident. It was surprisingly uncomfortable at first. I had already spoken about it from the stage, in men's circles, on zoom calls with my group coaching clients, and with friends. I could feel her kindness and empathy as she listened intently, holding space for me. After the call with Michelle, I went into a mediative state of reflection to access my discomfit, and the fear of being judged was present, along with feelings of shame. During this process, the thought came to me that sometimes we don't ever heal our wounds entirely, and that's okay. I've accepted and made peace with my childhood and the different emotionally significant events that I experienced.

We can't change the events in our life, but we can change how we feel and interpret those experiences.

Here are three insights that I used to empower myself.

1. When you open up to family, don't expect them to empathize with your ordeal. It's like asking someone to imagine a rose, but they have never seen one, or asking your friend what an orange tastes like, but they have never tried one. Best to join men's circles or hire a professional for support. This doesn't mean that you shouldn't open up to your family but don't expect them to understand.
2. It's okay to lose ourselves before we find ourselves. It's necessary to cut yourself some slack. Being self-critical is deadly to self-growth and healing. Look for things to be grateful for and try praising yourself. I make it a habit to congratulate myself often and for the littlest of things too. There is no escaping you, so you might as well be your own best friend.
3. Take all the things that you wish were different or that you don't like about yourself and make a list and state the opposite as an affirmation. For example, sometimes, I wish I had a more muscular body. Instead of hating my body, I can say I love and accept myself just the way I am. And make weights a part of my exercise routine. Affirmations are a great way to affirm the road you want to take in your life.

* * *

Here are some of my favourites:

- The things that I create are even better than I imagine them to be.
- I appreciate all that I am and all that I have.
- I allow myself to think and dream in unlimited ways.
- My choices, possibilities, and opportunities are expanding every day.
- The universe is safe, abundant and friendly.
- I always listen to the wisdom of my heart.
- I attract the highest and best in all people.
- Everything I do adds beauty, harmony, order and light to the universe.
- I allow myself to have more than I ever dreamed possible.

I WANT YOU TO KNOW

There are still bad days but we can be there for each other
You might lose all trust, including your trust in yourself
But trust your instincts and gut feelings
It was not your fault. You did not deserve it
Please come forward. Find your voice and tell your story
Make sure that you keep growing
You have so much to offer this world
You are strong, you are loved
There will be days where you don't believe this
Know that you have the strength to get through anything
Know that your body belongs to you
Their actions are not your fault. Abuse does not define you
When you feel lost or get stuck, be grateful, ask for help, find love, and give it warmth
Find a balance it's essential
Learn about mental health, how the brain works and stores information
Cry your eyes out. Do it in love and in pain
Practice presence. Find a movement practice.
Processing your emotions needs movement. Practice your new practice
Get as strong as fuck. Get grounded.
Show up for yourself. Keep going.
Hang in there, you will do amazing things.

NOTES

1. A BOY FROM KALANGADOO

1. Nelson, Portia (1993), *There's a Hole in my Sidewalk: The Romance of Self-Discovery*, reprinted with the permission of Beyond Words/Atria Books, a division of Simon & Schuster, Inc.

5. FINDING FREEDOM

1. Anthony Bourdain, celebrity chef, was best known for his culinary writings and television presentations. On June 8, 2018, Bourdain died by suicide while on location in France.

17. LINE IN THE SAND

1. Taylor, S. Caroline (2004), *Surviving the legal system : a handbook for adult & child sexual assault survivors & their supporters*, Coulomb Communications

19. THE DANCER

1. Campbell, Joseph (1990), *The hero's journey : the world of Joseph Campbell*, Harper & Row

ACKNOWLEDGMENTS

Projects such as this book do not come about on their own or without assistance, and we would like to thank the Victorian Centres Against Sexual Assault (CASA) and Survivors & Mates Support Network (SAMSN) for their advice and support.

We thank the members of Restoring Hope who brought these stories together and strived to ensure the authors' works had the opportunity to be published by identifying GCASA to take-up the mantle.

We also want to thank Shooting Star Press who have been instrumental in bringing this book to fruition.

To the many supporters of our authors, family members, friends and partners, psychologists, psychiatrists, coaches, and the many other personal and professional individuals that have, and continue, to support these men. Thank you not only for helping them in their healing, but for the example you set and the encouragement this gives others.

Most importantly, thank you to the men who have brought this book to life. It has been an honour to have you open your hearts and minds to share such an intimate perspective of your journey. Always remember that in standing strong in your convictions that you make a difference.

Valerie Prokopiv
Chair
GCASA

In memory of Tina Vercillo
Restoring Hope President, Rest in Peace, 2022

www.ingramcontent.com/pod-product-compliance
Lightning Source LLC
Chambersburg PA
CBHW041140110526
44590CB00027B/4077